Viking Knits and Ancient Ornaments

elsebeth lavold

Viking Knits and Ancient Ornaments

interlace patterns from around the world in modern knitwear

photography by anders rydell

Search Press

The frontispiece shows an interpretation of Viking age dragon ornamentations.
The dragons appear to study an illustration from a Spanish 11th century manuscript,
Commentary on the Apocalypse *by* Saint Beatus of Liébana.
Drawings by Elsebeth Lavold, composite by Anders Rydell.

First published in Great Britain in 2014 by
Search Press Limited, Wellwood, North Farm Road,
Tunbridge Wells, Kent TN2 3DR

First paperback edition 2019

Also published in the United States of America in 2014 by
Trafalgar Square Books
North Pomfret, Vermont 05053

ISBN: 978-1-78221-775-6

Photography: © Anders Rydell
Designs, artwork and charts: © Elsebeth Lavold
Graphic design: Anders Rydell, interior; RM Didier, jacket
Technical editing and translation: Carol Huebscher Rhoades

10 9 8 7 6 5 4 3 2 1

Contents

Foreword: A Small World of Infinite Size 7

Follow the Threads 8

Read This Before You Knit 13
    About the Patterns 13
    Sizes and Making Changes 13
    Gauge 13
    Yarns and Needles 13
    Pattern References 14
    Elsebeth Lavold Designer's Choice Yarns 14
    Care 14
    Errors 14

Loops 15
    Wing Loops 20
    Twisted Loops 26
    Rusila 29
    Vendel Loop 32
    Herkja 34
    Lillbjärs 37
    Osk 40

Rings & Chains 43
    Rings 44
    Chains 48
    Tova 50
    Twisted Rings 53
    Signild 57
    Looped Rings 62
    Fulla 68
    Heidrun 71
    Bjärs 74
    Oddrun 76

Little Knot and Fourknot 80
    Little Knot 80
    Lofn 86
    Fourknot 89
    Jord 92
    Fourknot, Little Knot and Swastika 96

Threeknot 97
   Eir.. 100
   Elisif... 104
   Fyrunga 110

Overhand Knot 113
   Dalby 118
   Kata 120

S-hook 126
   Arnhild.. 132
   Hofvarpnir 136
   Jarnsaxa 139
   S-hook Horizontal 142
   Disa 145

Braiding 148
   Two bands 148
   Three bands 152
   Four bands 153
   Langlif..156
   Six bands 158
   Mist 164
   Unn 170
   Unn child's sizes 172

The Grammar of Viking Cables 176
Abbreviations 178
Creating Cable Patterns 179
Technical Information.. 184
Reading Charts 186
Chart Symbols 187
The Lifted Increases used in Viking Knits Designs................ 188
The Patterns 189
Acknowledgements.. 190
My Heartfelt Thanks...191

A Small World of Infinite Size

Ever since my *Viking Patterns for Knitting* book was first published in 1998, I have continued to work with Viking age patterns and interlace. This ornamental treasure has in no way lost its appeal, neither for me, nor for the many knitters and others who have come into contact with them. For me, the project has actually grown and become increasingly multifaceted.

The *Knitting Along the Viking Trail* exhibition has toured Sweden, Denmark and the USA, and I have shown Viking Knits designs in a number of other contexts: in books, in Knitter's Magazine and Vogue Knitting, to name a few publications, when attending knitting symposiums, while giving lectures and workshops, in participating in handicraft exhibitions and even on a conference about the relevance of Viking culture in our time... It wouldn't be an exaggeration to say that I have been pretty entangled with the Vikings, as well as with my knitting, in the fifteen plus years that have passed.

In those years, I have frequently encountered people who have commented on the patterns and told of similar patterns they have seen when traveling, or in some cases in their homeland, and this planted the seed to what was to become this book. I started examining more thoroughly and systematically where else on this planet people are fascinated by the decorative powers of interlace patterns, and how they express this fascination in their arts and crafts. The quest became more exciting than I could ever have imagined.

In my typical manner, I started out in a rather unstructured way. As an avid cable knitter, I had a fair bit of knowledge about Celtic ornamentation, and I suspected that Islam, with its ban on realistic imagery of living beings, might produce interesting ornamental results; those were the first two lines of thought I pursued. I flipped through all the art books on the shelves of the Stockholm Public Library (and there are quite a few of them) to see if any interesting interlace patterns would turn up. And they certainly did, providing some additional threads in the pattern web of the ornamental universe I was about to explore.

I went on to visit other libraries and museums, both real world and virtual, and I naturally searched the Internet, looking at websites in every language I could make sense of, and some where I had to get help from friends and relatives to figure out the written content. From this platform I could search for, read about, look at and learn more about my new project.

I have mainly studied objects and images of objects with interlace ornamentation. Do they just emerge spontaneously in a given culture, or could there have been contact between the originators, spreading the inspirational ideas? I had to dig deep into history to satisfy my curiosity and try to understand what might have happened, and how. This was the beginning of a journey through a multitude of cultures that, for a period of some five hundred to a thousand years, shared a strong partiality to interlace patterns, with some of them having been in documented contact with each other. This line of thought is further developed in the *Follow the Threads* chapter, but I must emphasize that this is not a scientific dissertation, but rather my personal interpretation of an extensive but not detailed research.

Most cultures don't seem to attribute any specific symbolic meaning to the patterns, at least not beyond the obvious, such as creating ties between e.g. people or clans or undoing such ties. But as you will see in the following chapters, there are some pretty compelling exceptions to this rule.

Throughout my adult life, my love for needles and yarn, and their potential to expand our common ornamental heritage, has been the motivating factor to dig deeper into the technical aspects of knitting. Through the work of myself and others, Viking age decorative traditions are still relevant today, and are becoming "public domain" in a similar manner as their Celtic "cousins".

In the book, I analyze a great number of patterns and motifs; some from the Vikings, some Irish, and yet some from other parts of the world. I hope and believe that the simple but versatile technique I developed to create Viking Knits will extend into other ornamental traditions, making new designs possible, and inspiring people to develop their own patterns. You may start by joining me as I follow the threads of interlace through history and geography in the pages to come. I hope you will have as fun a ride as I have had, and still have.

Spånga, Sweden, February 2014
Elsebeth Lavold

Follow the Threads

Tying was the first technique man developed to keep things together. Ropes were twined and used in just about every aspect of primitive life; to carry home bundles of firewood, to secure the posts keeping your roof over your head, to weave baskets for storing and what not. Innumerable knots and braids were developed through the course of history, and it is safe to conclude that awareness of how threads can travel has been a human trait since the dawn of man. In the process of tying, twisting and weaving, the decorative potential becomes obvious.

There are ancient examples of using braided and twisted patterns for sheer decorative purposes. Among the oldest, dating back some eight thousand years, are objects found in present day Turkey: A knife handle ornamented with an S-hook depicting a serpent, and a basic twist on a clay stamp. To generally attribute serpent symbolism to patterns of this type is a very reasonable conclusion, as indicated by several examples in the S-hook chapter of this book.

The Vikings and their partiality to the decorative powers of interlace patterns were the ones who originally inspired me to embark on the ornamental journey that has resulted in this book. Well, it was not *just* the Vikings, but also the peoples of what Swedish historians refer to as the Vendel era, (550 to 800 AD, while the Viking Age spans from 800 to the mid-11th century AD), who can also claim to be inventors of patterns that have inspired me. But they too had their predecessors, as I was about to find out.

The 4th and 5th centuries AD, in the beginning of what has been named the Migration period, were years of great turmoil in Europe. By the end of the 4th century, Mongol hordes invaded eastern parts of Europe, forcing many Germanic peoples to abandon their homes. Goths migrated southward from Scandinavia through Eastern Europe, and the so called Visigoths eventually settled in present day Spain via Turkey, Greece and Italy, while the other major branch, the Ostrogoths, found a home in Italy and Austria. Vandals and other Germanic tribes made their way through Europe. Angles and Saxons left southern Denmark and northern Germany for the British Isles, and the Franks established a kingdom in, you guessed it, present day France. The remains of Roman rule, the Eastern Roman Empire, occupied what we now call Turkey and Greece. This intense mobility caused peoples and cultures to interact in both war and peace to an unprecedented extent.

Scandinavian decorative interlace originates from the earlier Germanic tradition of animal ornaments. It, in turn, may have been influenced by the invading Mongols. After the collapse of the Roman Empire, the Germanic tribes gained increased power, which also increased the status and distribution of their decorative preferences.

Langobards is the name of a semi-mythical Germanic tribe that, according to the sparse sources of information I have found, are claimed to have their roots in Scandinavia. (Throughout this book, I use the term "Langobards" instead of the more common English name "Lombards", which *can* mean the same thing, but also refers to inhabitants of present day Lombardy in Italy, some of which may be decendants of "my" Langobards, others not. By using terms like "Langobards" and "Langobardic" I'm simply pointing to a pre-medieval ornamental tradition, which is what *I'm* interested in, and I hope I don't offend any scholars by doing so.) The actuality of the Langobards seems to be held in doubt in some academic circles, while other historians attest to their existence. They are believed to have migrated south through Eastern Europe to reach present day Croatia by the 7th century, where a great number of decorated friezes and other stonemasonry with interlace patterns from that period have been found.

Some sources claim this type of ornamentation to be typical of Croatia, others that it is Langobardic. If there were artifacts of this type predating the arrival of the Langobards, a Levantine origin might be possible; the Middle East is not far from Croatia. But either way stonemasonry seems to have begun in Croatia at this very point in history.

The Langobards later continued westward and founded the north Italian region of Lombardy in the 11th century. Still to be found in Lombardy is an abundance of stonemasonry in the same style, and quite a few are shown in this book to illustrate various patterns. These borders and friezes may be the result of both Langobards getting access to types of stone which were easy to tool, and of coming into contact with Comacines, stonemasons already established in Lombardy. During the Langobardic invasion, the Comacines created what with present day terminology would be called an underground resistance movement. They communicated using secret signs carved into stones, and some believe that this is the origin of the Freemason organization. Be that as it may, Comacines and Langobards eventually merged into becoming Lombards and spread their ornamental culture all over Europe, actually as far as to the Cathedral in Lund in southern Sweden. It's a bit ironic that I have seen plenty of their work first-hand in both Italy and Croatia, but not in the country where I live. But it takes roughly twice the time to go by car from Stockholm to Lund than to take a plane from Stockholm to Lombardy; that's 21st century migration patterns for you.

In Saint Gall, Switzerland, not far from one of the principal Langobardic settlements in Lombardy, an abbey was founded in the 8th century. At the time, abbeys were important centers for preserving and spreading knowledge. This was long before the invention of printing, and all books were written and copied by hand. Among those who came to the abbey were Irish monks, and many of the manuscripts they produced can still be found today in the abbey archives. This is a source of some very appealing patterns, and thus referenced in my book.

Christianity reached Ireland already in the 5th century. Christian beliefs emanated from the numerous abbeys that were founded not only in Ireland, but also in Celtic parts of the British Isles, with the Abbey of Iona being one of the most well-known. Many English monks and noblemen came to the abbeys to study, and Irish missionaries brought their knowledge not only to England, but onto the continent, to France, to Visigoth Spain and to… Saint Gall.

Historical threads ran in the other direction as well: In the turbulent centuries of the Migration Period, from around 400 to 600 AD, the Irish abbeys became sanctuaries for continental scholars, where the producing and copying of manuscripts, primarily Christian in content, continued.

In the late 7th century, the ornamental style we have come to identify as "Celtic" emerged. However, the style itself is not Celtic. The early Celts were not into interlace patterns; their preferred ornamentation was spirals. A more recent, and better, name for this intricate interlace style is "insular", from the Latin word for island, since it was shared with the Anglo-Saxons of the British Isles. The style seems to have originated in the adornment of illuminated manuscripts and later spread to metal and stone works; the oldest stones with this type of ornamentation are said to be from the 9th century.

In time, this coincides with the first Viking raids. By the end of the 8th century, Norwegian Vikings began to pillage Ireland, followed by Danish Vikings attacking England. Abbeys were obvious targets, filled, as they were, with gold and other valuables. Some Vikings decided to remain, and parts of their culture were integrated with the Celts and Anglo Saxons. The Vikings who did return to Scandinavia brought with them both influences and actual objects. An exchange of culture between these three peoples has undoubtedly taken place. Vikings also sailed up the River Seine to Paris, as well as along the Atlantic coastline of Portugal and Spain and into the Mediterranean. However, these journeys have not left as clear a mark in terms of artifacts and influences as the westbound travels.

The Swedish Vikings of the same period steered east and south, to Russia, down the River Volga eventually reaching Constantinople, present day Istanbul in Turkey. Already by the mid-9th century, Swedish Vikings had found their way into the Byzantine Empire, the Middle East successor of the Roman Empire, where some of them enlisted as mercenaries. They came as far as Bagdad, at the time the capital of the Muslim world. They were not able to establish settlements in this region, probably because they faced such a well-organized society, but we know they traded slaves and furs. This is another example of cultural exchange taking place well over a thousand years ago.

The Middle East has a truly ancient tradition of interlace ornamentation. It can be found on pottery and clay stamps from Babylonia, Mesopotamia and Assyria dating back to millennia before we started counting our years, and interlace is also found on stone reliefs and mosaics from Classic Antiquity, the Roman and Byzantine Empires. When Christianity emerged, the Christian church became an element in the spread pattern of decorative interlace.

In Syria, a specialized written language was created to spread the Word. It was used in magnificent colorful manuscripts with interlace ornamented pages reminiscent of the prayer rugs employed in early Christian worship practices. These manuscripts became widespread, and served as a source of inspiration for the aforementioned insular manuscripts. In the third century, Armenia emerged as a Christian kingdom. The first king allegedly had a vision of a Christian cross and immediately converted. This is a part of Armenian tradition that constitutes the very foundation of its Christian identity; the Armenian culture has no pre-Christian history. These stories were laid down in writing in early 6th century Syria, at about the same time as the Syriac written language was created.

Unique to Armenia are the so called Khatchkars, carved stone reliefs, primarily used as grave stones or memorials. The oldest date back to the 10th century, but the tradition reached its peak in the 14th century. The motifs are generally crosses adorned with sophisticated interlace of a kind typical of Armenian art.

In Egypt, the Copts (Christian Egyptians) excelled in the production of incredible woven and embroidered textiles, an amazing number of which have survived to present day as garments and fragments dating from 600–800 AD and onward. Many of them include braided band ornaments.

To the ancient Egyptians, the Ankh served as a symbol of eternal life. The Copts further developed the Ankh shape into a type of cross that appears to have been a model for the Celtic cross. A Coptic type cross appears on a Coptic grave slab from the 7th century, at least a century before corresponding cross shapes appear in Scotland and Ireland.

Thus, so far we have Celts in contact with Copts and Vikings in both Bagdad and Constantinople. Food for thought, don't you think…?

Early in Christian history, in the 4th century, a Christian enclave emerged in Aksum in Ethiopia, possibly as a result of contact with the Copts. The Kingdom of Aksum was an influential trading nation from the 1st to the 9th century. The Aksumites used interlace to decorate their churches and processional crosses, one of which has found its way into the pages this book. In general shape, the processional crosses originate from the Coptic cross.

In early the 7th century, merchant and Prophet Muhammad began preaching the Word of God, and by the time the Vikings reached Bagdad, the Muslim Empire was already strong and far-reaching. The Islamic ban on depicting living creatures paved the way for an extensive use of geometrical patterns. In early Islamic tradition, interlace occurs adorning both buildings and works of art, from India and Iran in the east to Morocco and Spain in the west. Many of the patterns are closely related to the ones used by Vikings and Celts, and the oldest stem from the early 9th century. Stone reliefs are common in the oldest Islamic monuments, a continuation of the Roman-Byzantine tradition. In Spain, you can find three stone sarcophagi, superficially very similar but considered to be made in three distinct styles, Mozarabic (European Muslim), Visigoth and Roman.

In addition to their use in early Christianity, prayer rugs are employed in Islam as well, and there are holy Islamic manuscript pages reminiscent in their design of such rugs, just as in their aforementioned Christian counterparts. It seems to me that early Islamic art was subject to the same Coptic and eastern Mediterranean influences as the Insular culture in the British Isles.

As mentioned above, the Goths that were exiled by the 4th century Hun invasion split into an Ostrogoth tribe, settling in Italy, and the Visigoths, ruling the Iberian Peninsula and southern France. Both tribes developed a strong tradition of interlace ornamentation that may have been influenced by visiting Irish seafarers. When the Muslims invaded Spain in the 8th century, they brought with them their Islamic interlace tradition, in turn probably influenced by Roman and/or Insular culture. So Spain is the likely meeting ground for east and west, since the Irish didn't reach as far east as to the Middle East until the 9th century. Visigoth interlace styles seem to have upheld their presence in Spain even after the Muslims had left. And it's not entirely unlikely that the interlace patterns found in eastern France could have been subject to Langobardic influence.

Have you reached the point where my many threads become tangled in your mind? If so, I don't blame you, and don't forget that I allow myself elements of speculation here, intertwined with the historic facts. But one fact clearly stands out: In the early Medieval days, interlace was a type of ornamentation that was immensely popular in the entire cultural sphere of Europe, only to essentially lose appeal around the turn of the last millennium. But in the "golden era of interlace patterns", influences traveled back and forth between various local varieties, cross-breeding and evolving, even if it's impossible to pinpoint exactly who influenced whom and at what point in time. But having spent years and years of trying to probe into the designer minds of my Viking ancestors, and having learnt a thing or two in the process, I believe that the hints are there to be found in the artifacts. And there are plenty of interesting ornamental traditions to explore outside of Europe as well.

The Huns invading Europe in the 5th century were Mongols. With their strong tradition as horsemen, thus coming into daily contact with things like bridles, I find it highly likely that interlace was a part of their ornamental tradition, in addition to twining leather bands for practical purposes. The 13th century saw another Mongol invasion, this time in the Middle East. If these Mongols weren't already familiar with interlace patterns, they certainly had every opportunity to bring such patterns back home. A Mongol tribe called Khalka, who consider themselves descendants of Genghis Khan, have developed and refined exquisite interlace typically found on leather and silver objects, and drawings of a few of those have made their way into this book.

The Islamic expansion to the south brings us to Benin and Nigeria, where we find a highly developed interlace tradition in wood carvings, bronze objects and beadworks. There are archaeological finds that date back to the 12th century, but the tradition is probably even older, later to be further supported as a result of Islamic influences. The Yoruba people were particularly skilled in both bronze works and bone and wood carving. Similar motifs are found on embroidered shirts made by the Nigerian Hausa people.

Further south, I have had reason to study several tribes in the kingdom of Kuba in present day Democratic Republic of Congo: the Bakuba, the Shoowa and their neighbors the Bushongo. Their traditions show all the signs of being indigenous, and their sophisticated interlace is put to widespread use; among the most spectacular are the embroidered ceremonial textiles that have become known as Kasai velvets. Tradition and climate are the main reasons why few traditional Kasai velvets have survived into present day, and most of those are found in European collections. The oldest date back to the 17th and 18th centuries. Other uses include beadwork, carved wooden boxes, body decorations like tattoos and scaring, and adorning buildings. Their interlace patterns are among the most unique in the world, combining geometrical precision with variation and repetitive and rhythmic use of similar but not identical pattern elements.

The Youruba, the Hausa and the Kuba all use the word "imbol" or "ibo" to indicate a pattern where one line crosses another and then returns to the beginning in an uninterrupted loop motif. These braided and endless motifs are said to represent the continuity and balance we need in our lives.

Apart from the Mongol interlace, patterns of this kind are sparse in Asia. However, the Fourknot is frequent in Japanese, Chinese and Tibetan art, where it is a symbol of luck or fortune. The Buddhist Eternal Knot is a braided knot of the same kind as on many Viking objects, and many Asian cultures share the belief that the Eternal Knot brings good fortune. India provides examples mainly in a traditional form of street painting, referred to as Kolam in the south and Rangoli in the north of India, and predominantly making use of the Little Knot, the Fourknot and intricate variations of the swastika. Indian textiles sometimes display S-hooks. Apart from the above, I have been unable to find examples of braids, twists or other interlaced motifs anywhere else in Asia. The peoples of Oceania and the subarctic regions also seem totally devoid of interlace in their decorative traditions, so I'm afraid I can't really claim that using interlace is something deeply rooted in human nature. Or can I, only there are exceptions to the general rule…?

North America is another part of the world where interlace has not been an element in the traditional "pattern library", with one exception: several Native American tribes in southeastern USA produced neck adornments known as "shell gorgets", typically with a pattern of a Fourknot and four woodpeckers. They were in use from around the mid-13th to the mid-15th century.

A few artifacts with interlace stem from Central America. The Maya culture, flourishing between 250 and 900 AD, has made use of a traditional Three Band Braid. The Little Knot, regarded as a symbol of movement and change, and basic twists are both part of the decorative tradition of the Aztecs, 1300–1500 AD.

Quite by lucky coincidence I found a small monograph about the people living in present day Suriname in the northeastern part of South America. Tribes of escaped African slaves have developed a tradition of carved household items, eating tools, combs and other such utensils, decorated with interlace patterns.

The Peruvian Chavin culture also displays some examples of interlace decorations, dating back to the first millennium BC.

If I had defined my quest, project, research, call it what you like, as one of finding *the* origin of ornamental braids, twists and knots, I would have to admit to failing. But this was never my objective. The fascination I felt in discovering how interlace ornamentation can be found in so many different cultures, some of them with documented or possible contact, and the interesting and unexpected find that the appeal of such patterns often seems to have had a limited lifespan, has been reward enough.

Another positive effect has been the inspiration for new knitwear designs the project has generated. And even though all the designs in this book have been given old Norse names, to keep my own tradition intact, I think you will find that Viking Knits encompasses a lot more than just the inspiration from the Vikings. With this book I can add Germanic peoples, Semites, Africans, Mongols, Native Americans and a whole lot of other pre-historic, historic and present-day fellow humans to the list of Fans of Interlace Ornamentation. And that, in turn, leads me to a very comforting conclusion: That the human race is really a tight knit community, with more things tying us together than separating us. Just follow the threads and I think you will agree.

A beautiful winged Little Knot on a Roman mosaic. The original can be seen at the Santa Giulia Museo, Brescia, Italy.

Read This Before You Knit

About the Patterns

Instructions are given for the smallest size followed by larger sizes in parentheses, separated by commas. When only one number is given, it applies to all sizes.

I have tried to keep the instructions short and clear. If you miss information, or something isn't clear, chances are the information can be found in the chapters on:

The Grammar of Viking Cables, p. 176

Technical Information, p. 184

Reading Charts, p. 186

The patterns are written so that everything happens on the right side (RS) unless otherwise specified.

Once you have done something, continue working as set until the next set of instructions. If a motif is placed on a piece, the sts on either side should be worked as before unless otherwise specified. For a more thorough discussion on how to read patterns, I refer to my website; *General Suppositions of Knitting Patterns or What a Knitter is Presumed to Know,* http://www.ingenkonst.se/needknow.htm

The instructions are kept fairly general. I leave it up to you to use your preferred ways of increasing and decreasing at points where the type and placement is not essential. If you want to know what I usually do, I suggest reading the technical section on p. 184—actually I recommend that you read it in any case.

Sizes and Making Changes

When I design, I use lists of measurements for ready-to-wear, but our bodies are different and we have different preferences concerning fit. When you select which size to knit, look at both my sizing and the actual measurements. You may prefer a tighter or looser fit than I intended and therefore prefer a size larger or smaller than your normal size.

Many of the garments can be shortened or lengthened. When the pattern is repeated in length, you can usually add 2 rows between repeats. These rows should be worked as they present themselves, knit on knit and purl on purl. When changing the length in this manner, you may have to adjust measurements before and after increases and de-creases and possibly (definitely for sleeve length) adjust the number of rows between increases or decreases. In many cases you can lengthen a garment by adding an extra repeat at the bottom. If you do, mark the end of that repeat and take your measurements from that point.

Gauge

Correct gauge is essential if you want the garment to have the correct measurements. Take the time to knit a swatch and check your gauge before starting a project! It will save time in the long run. Knit a 4 × 4 in / 10 × 10 cm square in stockinette stitch, that is the recommended gauge + edge sts. If the swatch is too small, change to larger needles; if it is too large, change to smaller needles. Be sure to check both stitch and row gauge. If the gauge in stockinette stitch corresponds to the gauge given in the pattern, the measurements of your garment will also correspond. The measurements for ribbing are based on stretching the ribbing to the gauge for stockinette.

Yarns and Needles

I have used yarns from my line of Elsebeth Lavold Designer's Choice yarns that I find most suitable for these designs. If you want to use yarn other than the one recommended, make sure that it works to the given gauge. Also, remember that fibers behave differently. Not only do different fibers have different qualities, but different grades of the same fiber will give different results. Swatch before substituting.

The yarn quantities are based on average requirements and may differ between knitters. If you substitute yarns, the amount required may differ, even when using a yarn of the same length per yards/meters. Consult with your store about how much to buy.

The suggested needle sizes are recommendations. Use whatever size is necessary to obtain the correct gauge. I generally give only needle sizes and leave it up to you to use straights or circulars.

A certain type of needle, such as double-pointed needles, will be specified only when necessary.

Continued

Pattern References

Nearly all the patterns in this book are genuinely new in the sense that they have never been knitted before (even if I frequently draw inspiration from, or even copy, design elements made in other techniques). Sometimes these new patterns are based on, or are variations of, patterns that I have previously analyzed, most often in the book that made my Viking Knits Project public: *Viking Patterns for Knitting*.

One of my ambitions with this book is to convey the "developmental logic" within each pattern group (see e.g. the chapter Creating Cable Patterns on p. 179), so when a pattern in this book is related to patterns in my previous writings, I mention it, knowing very well that most language editions of *Viking Patterns* are sold out and only available second hand. I could have included pages with previously published swatches and charts, but then this book would most likely have had to be more expensive and also serving "reruns" to owners of *Viking Patterns*. However, there isn't a single item, pattern element or design, that calls for access to *Viking Patterns* to knit, so I hope you don't mind these references to satisfy my own ambitions to structure and logic. In some cases, you can most probably deduct or recreate such "referred patterns" from the information supplied in this book, even if there isn't a swatch or a chart.

Elsebeth Lavold Designer's Choice Yarns

Here are the technical specifications for the yarns used:

Silky Wool   45% wool, 35% silk, 20% polyamide
192 yd/175 m / 50 g

Hempathy   41% cotton, 34% hemp, 25% modal
175 yd/160 m / 50 g

The following yarns were used to knit the original projects but have since been discontinued:

Silky Wool XL (80% wool, 20% silk; 104 yd/95 m / 50 g)
For designs knitted in Silky Wool XL, you can use Silky Wool held double and both the gauge and yarn amounts should remain the same. You could also use *Misty Wool* (75% wool / 25% hemp, 100 g = 230 yd / 210 m). It works to the same gauge as Silky Wool XL, but you will need less yarn.

Favorite Wool (100% Peruvian wool; 109 yd/100 m / 50 g)
My suggestion for a substitute yarn is *Heaven's Hand Wool Classic* from Cornelia Hamilton, which has identical specifications and properties. *Misty Wool* would also work well.

SensuAl (98% baby alpaca, 2% polyamide; 88 yd/80 m / 50 g)
This yarn is used for a scarf; any reasonably soft wool or wool blend yarn will serve as a substitute. A tighter gauge will result in a narrower scarf, and a looser gauge will result in a wider scarf. Talk to your local yarn store about how much yarn you'll need.

LinSilk (50% linen, 30% viscose, 20% silk; 219 yd/200 m / 100 g)
I have no suggestion for an ideal substitute to offer, but any blend of cotton or linen with silk or bamboo should work well if the length per weight is in the same range and it knits up to a similar gauge.

ViSilk (90% viscose, 10% silk; 132 yd/120 m / 50 g)
My suggestion for a substitute yarn is *Heaven's Hand Sister Silk* from Cornelia Hamilton (100% mulberry silk, 131 yd/120 m / 50 g). The yarn amounts should be the same.

Elsebeth Lavold Designer's Choice yarns are produced for and distributed in the USA by Knitting Fever Inc. For information about retailers, please use the store locator at **www.knittingfever.com**.

Care

Do not wash garments unnecessarily. Instead, air garments often—it's better for you, better for the garment, and better for the environment. Turn the garment inside out before washing. Check the ball band for washing instructions. Hand washing in cool to lukewarm water is recommended for most yarns. Always use a mild detergent. Do not soak. For all yarns containing wool, rinse in the same temperature water as for washing. Do not wring. Instead, short spin in a washing machine (without water) or roll in a towel and press out water. Do not leave wet. Reshape and dry flat away from heat or direct sunlight. Use a damp pressing cloth over the garment when pressing. Do not store knitted garments hanging.

Errors

We have taken all possible precautions to avoid errors. If you discover an error that has slipped past our pattern check, please send an email to **info@ingenkonst.se** *and we will post a correction on our website* **www.ingenkonst.se**.

Loops

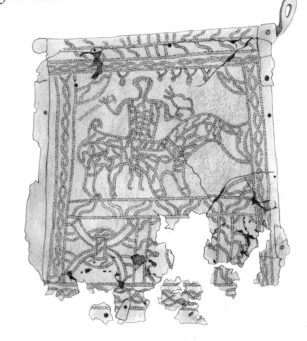

The essence of Viking ornamentation is bands traveling across a background, and the most basic pattern you can make with a band is a loop. The Vikings made a lot of loops, and also typically made the bands twist and turn in a variety of other ways, and not very systematically at that.

Numerous rune stones, scattered all over the central parts of Sweden, show examples of this spirited looping. The one in the photo below has been used as a building block in a wall of the church in Kårsta, some 25 miles north of Stockholm, centuries after Sven carved the loops (yes, he has actually signed his work, as did many of his stone carving colleagues).

The Odal rune in the Elder Futhark (the rune alphabet) is just such a basic loop. Odal is a Germanic word meaning "inheritance" or "inherited estate", and the shape itself is usually interpreted as a symbol of real property. The depicted weather vane from the Stockholm suburb Grimsta, very close to my home, is decorated with a series of loops just above the horse and rider.

The basic loop can be oriented four ways; up, down, left and right. Variations of each orientation also emerge depending on which band is on top of the other where they cross. Only one such variation is shown here; the other is made by changing the direction of all the cable crossings across stockinette bands. Be sure to systematically keep track of the over-under sequence.

The Bushongo people of the Kuba Kingdom in present day Congo have used all four orientations, letting the "legs" of the loops intertwine on a raphia embroidery (right). Danish Vikings thought the loop made a pretty motif side by side with a Figure Eight on this small bead found in Gram (below right). The Aucaner tribe in Suriname placed the loop on a "food paddle" (eating tool, below left), and their Saramaccan neighbors used it to decorate a stool (top right).

Serpent décor on a wooden stool, Saramaccan tribe, Suriname

Kasai Velvet fabric, Kuba tribe, Congo

Above left: Food paddle, Aucaner tribe, Suriname
Above right: Gold bead, Gram, Denmark

Upwards Pointing Loop (Odal Rune)

Downwards Pointing Loop

Loops pointing up and down can be used as separate motifs, but can also be made attached to bands by skipping row 1 and 3 for the upwards pointing and row 19 and 20 for the downwards pointing loop. This creates a variety of ways to use loops as pattern design elements.

12 sts (16 sts)

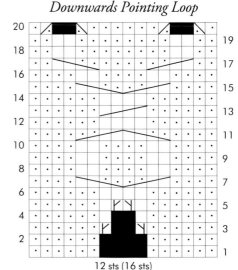

12 sts (16 sts)

Left: Initial from Book of Kells, Ireland
Below left: Wooden cup, Kuba, Congo
Below: Ethiopian Lalibela Cross

A multitude of interlace patterns can be seen in the initial from the beautiful illuminated manuscript Gospel *The Book of Kells*. A row of loops appear above the letter A, but the design also includes a Four-band Cable, a Vendel Knot, an S-hook and a Multiple Knot. Wow, perhaps I was an Irish monk in a previous life.

A single loop is placed on a cup from the Congolese Kuba tribe. Twelve loops, thought to symbolize the twelve disciples, are placed along the periphery of a Lalibela Cross, a 16th century Ethiopian processional cross.

Make a vertical mirror image of the Odal rune and let the "legs" of the two intertwine to form a different and beautiful motif, as seen on the mount from Stavanger, Norway. In order to balance the motif, I had to make the loop larger in my knitted version.

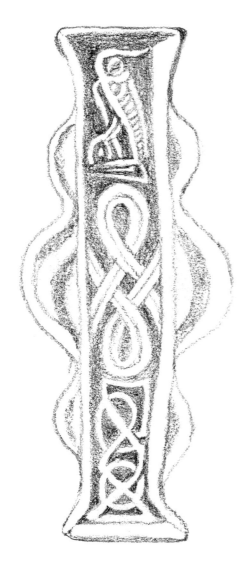

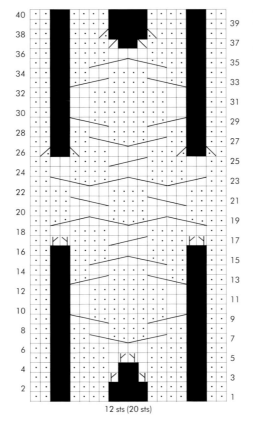

Above: Mount, Stavanger, Norway
Middle column: Braided Loops
Right: Nigerian bronze bracelet

If you let the "legs" of the loops meet, alternately pointing up and down, you create a Zigzag pattern with the loops placed where the bands turn. This pattern is widely spread and appreciated. A Viking age interpretation can be seen on the buckle from Stenkyrka, Gotland, Sweden, while the Nigerian arm ring below is an example of the global appeal of the pattern. The photo of an Italian stone, probably Langobardic, displays the panel together with several other interesting patterns. If you remember the days when we were most often sitting down bound to a cord when talking on the phone, quite a few of us would doodle, and in the process frequently create a looped zigzag pattern, as if there was a direct link between our subconscious ornamental brain and our hand. To me, having done some probing into the therapeutic effects of knitting, this is a fascinating factoid.

12 sts (20 sts)

Above: Viking age brooch from Sten-kyrka, Gotland, Sweden
Right: Late 8th or early 9th century stone fragment from the Basilica of Santa Maria Assunta, now in Museo Archeologico Nazionale di Cividale del Friuli, Italy

As mentioned on the previous page, in addition to pointing up and down, loops can be tilted left or right. However, the tilted versions cannot be knitted as isolated pattern elements; they need to find their starting point in a vertical band, a border or from another motif. For that reason I refer to them as "Wing Loops"—the loops resemble wings when placed together. The ornamentation on the bowl of a Viking Age spoon from Sigtuna, Sweden (below) is a good example.

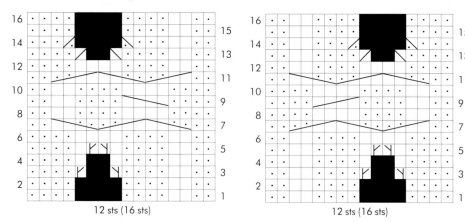

Wing Loops Left & Right

Wing Loop variations shown here are
  a) with the bands forming a classic cable,

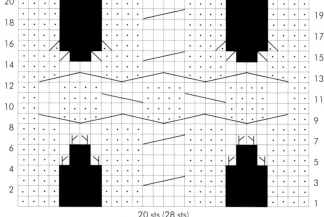

b) attached to crossing bands, and

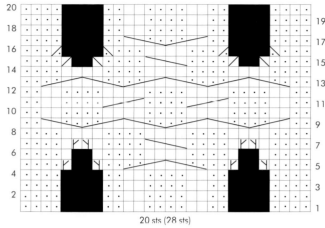

20 sts (28 sts)

c) placed together with the bands cut to create an isolated motif.

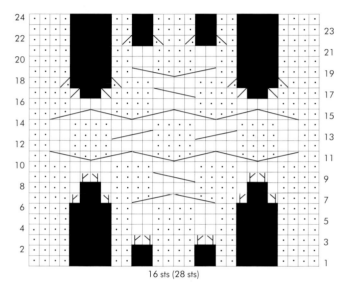

16 sts (28 sts)

Pairs of Wing Loops, corresponding to one repeat of the Wing Loops on Bands pattern, are used in the bottom ornament of the entrance to the mausoleum of Ashik Pasha, a Turkish poet and Sufi. He pioneered writing poetry in Ottoman Turkish, and the mausoleum was built shortly before his death in 1333, while Turkey was still under Mongol rule. Several other interesting patterns can be seen on the façade, among them a Two Band Twist and the Skabersjö border, analyzed in my *Viking Patterns for Knitting* book. The Congolese Bushongo people provide another example in one of their raphia embroideries (below), and the Wing Loop motif adorns a Nigerian salt cellar (not shown).

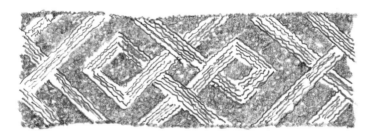

Instead of placing the loops adjacent to each other as in the preceding patterns, you can stagger them vertically. I don't think I'm the only one to see a serpent in this shape, see for example the image of the serpent god Apep from inside an Egyptian pyramid. Or is the Meigle mermaid on the Pictish stone actually a serpent goddess? Her looped tails are pretty nevertheless. As used on the picture stone from Martingbo, Gotland, Sweden and the Croatian Langobardic carved stone, the purpose is probably simply aesthetic rather than symbolical.

Vertical Zigzag Loops

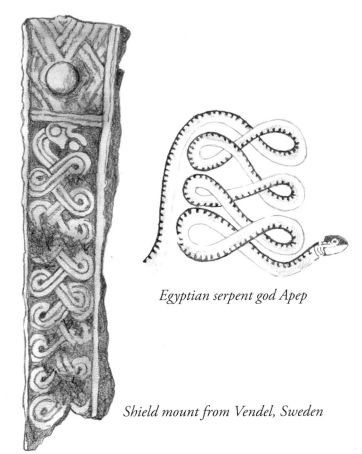

Egyptian serpent god Apep

Shield mount from Vendel, Sweden

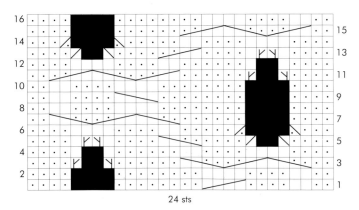

24 sts

The Pictish Meigle mermaid

On the Croatian stone, it looks as if the loops line up, but this is because the right diagonal has been made steeper than the left; something which is not possible to achieve in knitting.

On yet another embroidered fabric from the Congolese Kuba people a braided variety is used as a surface pattern, and a Croatian folk art embroidery provides a horizontal example along with other wing loop elements (not shown).

Above: Rune stone from Martingbo, Gotland, Sweden
Right: Fragment of a 9ᵗʰ century marble tablet, on display in Muzej Lapidarium, Novigrad, Croatia

In Celtic ornamentation, it is the loops instead of the legs that are intertwined to form braided patterns; a configuration that can be seen in many medieval manuscripts. In the manuscripts this type of border is generally placed horizontally, but in knitting only the vertical orientation comes out looking good. The distance between Braided Wing Loops is easy to adjust by simply making the bands between them shorter or longer.

Braided Wing Loops

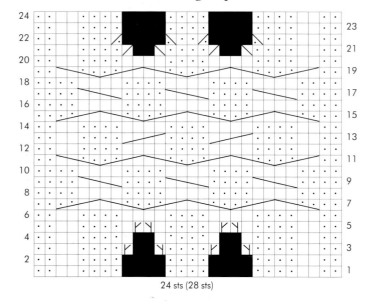

24 sts (28 sts)

*Intriguing Initial (It's an "I")
from the famous Illuminated Irish
manuscript The Book of Kells*

Stone frieze from the cathedral in Pisa, Italy

In a small beautiful corner decoration of an Irish manuscript from the Abbey of Saint Gall, Switzerland, two bands of Twisted Wing Loops are joined zipper-style and closed at each end with a double overhand knot. The drawing shows the central part of the border (right).

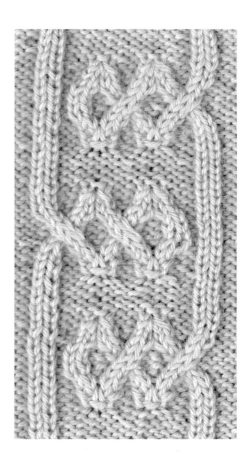

Wing Loops Twisted & Staggered

Marble pillar, Como, Italy,
on display in Musei Civici di Como

20 sts (28 sts)

Add the extra twist in a different manner and a new pattern is formed. The basic shape allows for four variations, turned left, right, up and down. Such Twisted Wing Loops are used in the border of the box-shaped brooch from Gotland, Sweden, and a quirky variation with an S-hook flanked by

Twisted Wing Loops appear on the mount from Björkö, Sweden, and also on the Langobardic stone frieze from Müstair, Switzerland. On the pommel of a sword from Pappilanmäki, Finland, a pair of mirrored Twisted Wing Loops can be seen (next spread).

Above left: Viking age brooch from Gotland, Sweden
Above right: Viking age mount from Björkö, Sweden
Below: Langobardic stone frieze, Müstair, Switzerland

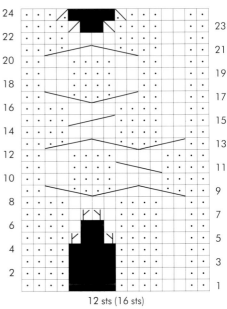

12 sts (16 sts)

Twisted Wing Loop Up Left

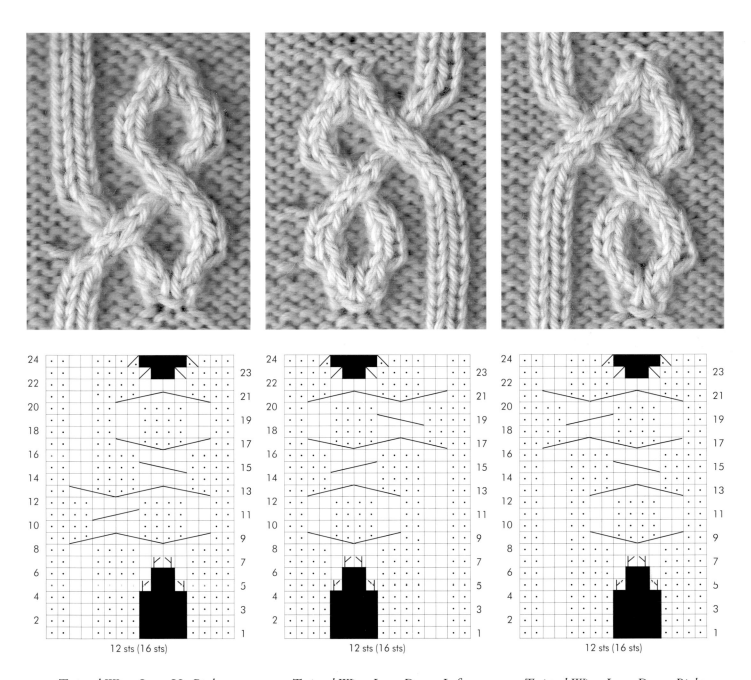

Twisted Wing Loop Up Right *Twisted Wing Loop Down Left* *Twisted Wing Loop Down Right*

I have not found any artifacts displaying these two variations with Mirrored Wing Loops on a Cable, but they are so pretty that I'm sure someone else must have discovered them too.

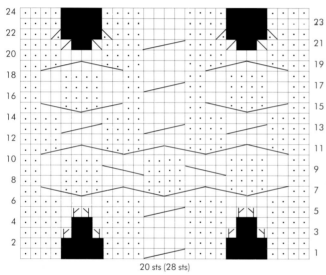

Twisted Wing Loops Up on Cable

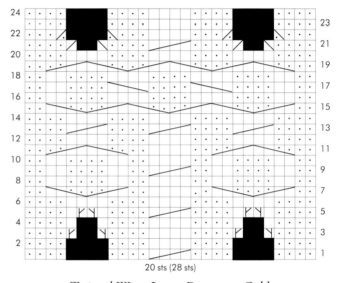

Twisted Wing Loops Down on Cable

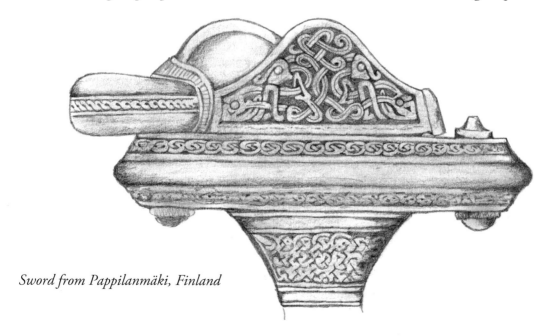

Sword from Pappilanmäki, Finland

RUSILA

This jacket has the ease of a Japanese kimono, but it is shaped around the shoulders for a more elegant fit. The dramatic cable pattern on the edging at the front is echoed on the cuffs, creating simplicity and drama in one garment.

The historic, however possibly fictional, Rusila fought against her brother Thrond for the thrones of both Denmark and Norway, at least according to Saxo Grammaticus' Gesta Danorum *(History of the Danes).*

Sizes   S (M, L, XL, XXL)

Finished measurements

Chest	37½ (41¼, 43¾, 47¾, 51½) in
	95 (105, 111, 121, 131) cm
Length	28¾ in
	73 cm

Materials

Yarn   Silky Wool XL (p. 14)

Yarn amounts   750 (800, 850, 900, 950) g

Needles   US size 8 / 5 mm, circular recommended
Cable needle

Gauge   17 sts × 24 rows in stockinette
= 4 × 4 in / 10 × 10 cm

Adjust needle size to obtain correct gauge if necessary.

Edge stitches The outermost st at each side is an edge st. Edge sts are included in the stitch counts and are always knitted unless otherwise specified.

Note Decrease inside the edge st when shaping front edge p. 184.

Charts Twisted Wing Loops Down on Cable p. 28.

Back

Cast on 93 (101, 107, 115, 123) sts and begin on WS. Work 5 rows k1, p1 ribbing (1st row begins with p1). Change to stockinette and decrease 1 st at each side on every 16th row 6 times = 81 (89, 95, 103, 111) sts. Continue without further shaping until piece is 21¼ (21, 20½, 20, 19¾) in / 54

(53, 52, 51, 50) cm long. Shape armholes by first binding off 3 (4, 5, 6, 7) sts and then 2 sts at each side. Next, decrease 1 st at each side on every other row 5 (6, 7, 8, 9) times = 61 (65, 67, 71, 75) sts. When armhole measures 8 (8¼, 8¾, 9, 9½) in / 20 (21, 22, 23, 24) cm, shape shoulders with short rows, beginning at neck edge: work until 6 (6, 7, 7, 9) sts remain; turn and work back until 6 (6, 7, 7, 9) sts remain. Turn and work the next 4 rows each 6 (7, 7, 8, 8) sts shorter. Bind off 25 sts for back neck and then, with a separate strand for each, bind off 18 (20, 21, 23, 25) sts for each shoulder.

Left Front

Cast on 81 (85, 89, 93, 97) sts and set up pattern.

Row 1, WS: Edge st, p4, k8, p4, k8, p4, (p1, k1) 26 (28, 30, 32, 34) times = 52 (56, 60, 64, 68) sts ribbing.

Row 2: Work knit over knit and purl over purl on ribbing and knit the last 29 sts for front edge.

Rows 3 and 5: Edge st, p4, k8, p4, k8, p4, work 52 (56, 60, 64, 68) sts ribbing.

Row 4: Work 52 (56, 60, 64, 68) sts ribbing, 2/2 RC, k8, 2/2 RC, k8, 2/2 RC, edge st.

Row 6: Now work 52 (56, 60, 64, 68) sts stockinette and k29 sts for front edge.

Row 7: Edge st, p4, k8, p4, k8, p4, work 52 (56, 60, 64, 68) sts stockinette.

Row 8: Work 52 (56, 60, 64, 68) sts stockinette, 2/2 RC, 20 sts following chart, 2/2 RC, edge st. The charted pattern is framed by two cables, continue crossing these cables every 4th row as set. Now begin decreasing 1 st at front edge with ssk inside inside 30 sts on every 8th row and, *at the same time,* decrease 1 st at side with k2tog every 16th row. Decrease at the side a total of 6 times and at the front a total of 18 (18, 19, 19, 19).

When piece measures 21¼ (21, 20½, 20, 19¾) in / 54 (53, 52, 51, 50) cm, shape armhole by first binding off 3 (4, 5, 6, 7) sts and then 2 sts at the side. Next, decrease 1 st at the side on every other row 5 (6, 7, 8, 9) times = 47 (49, 50, 52, 54) sts remain. When armhole measures 8 (8¼, 8¾, 9, 9½) in / 20 (21, 22, 23, 24) cm, shape shoulder with short rows, beginning at front edge: Work until 6 (6, 7, 7, 9) sts remain; turn and work back. Work the 29 sts of front edge + 6 (7, 7, 8, 8) sts; turn and work back. Using a separate strand, bind off 18 (20, 21, 23, 25) sts for the shoulder. Cast on a new edge st at the shoulder and continue in pattern. Shape the neckband with short rows, beginning at front edge after Rows 1, 5, 9, 13, 17, and 21. Work knit over knit and purl over purl to the center cable; turn and work back the same way. Work the next pattern row. After completing the last pattern repeat, bind off in pattern.

Right Front

Work as for left front, reversing shaping. Decrease inside 30 sts at the front with k2tog and with ssk at side. Begin short rows 1 row earlier and *before Rows* 1, 5, 9, 13, 17, and 21.

Sleeves

Cast on 60 sts and set up pattern:

Row 1, WS: Edge st, p4, k8, p4, k8, p4, k2, p4, k8, p4, k8, p4, edge st.

Row 2: Knit.

Row 3: = Row 1.

Row 4: Edge st, 2/2 RC, k8, 2/2 RC, k8, 2/2 RC, k2, 2/2 RC, k8, 2/2 RC, k8, 2/2 RC, edge st.

Work rows 1 and 2 once more and then begin working reverse stockinette between the cables. Cross the cables on every 4th row. After working the 2nd cable crossing, work following the chart between the outermost cables and the cables at the center (two times on the row). Continue crossing all cables in tandem with the center cable of the chart. Work 1 repeat + Rows 1 and 2.

Change to stockinette and, on the first stockinette row, work k2tog with the center 2 sts of every cable = 54 sts remain. Increase 1 st at each side on every 12th (10th, 8th, 6th, 4th) row 4 (6, 8, 10, 12) times = 62 (66, 70, 74, 78) sts. When sleeve is 15¾ in / 40 cm, long, shape sleeve cap by first binding off 3 (4, 5, 6, 7) sts and then 2 sts at each side. Next, decrease 1 st at each side on every other row until 28 sts remain. Bind off 3 sts at the beginning of every row 4 times. Bind off remaining 16 sts.

Finishing

Undo bound-off sts and join shoulders with three-needle bind-off.

Front bands: Pick up and knit 145 sts along left front, picking up 2 sts for every 3 rows. Knit 1 row, purl 1 row, knit 1 row. Bind off knitwise on RS. Work the right front band the same way. Seam short ends of front band at center back and then sew down band along back neck. Attach sleeves. Sew sleeve and side seams.

An uncommon but very interesting configuration is formed if you combine a regular loop with a skewed variety in a two-band pattern. It can be found on a few Viking artifacts, hence the name, but also on the depicted, possibly Langobardic, arch found in Rome, Italy.

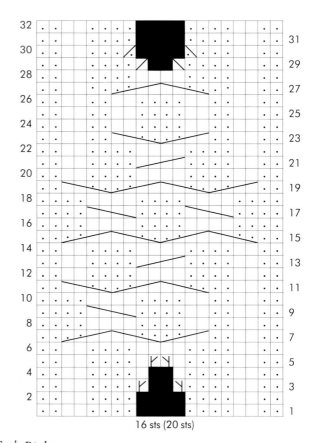

Building detail, Rome, Italy, believed to be Langobardic

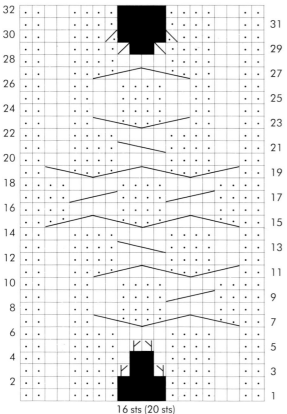

16 sts (20 sts)

16 sts (20 sts)

Vendel Loop Up Left & Right

The small loop can be made to point downwards as well:

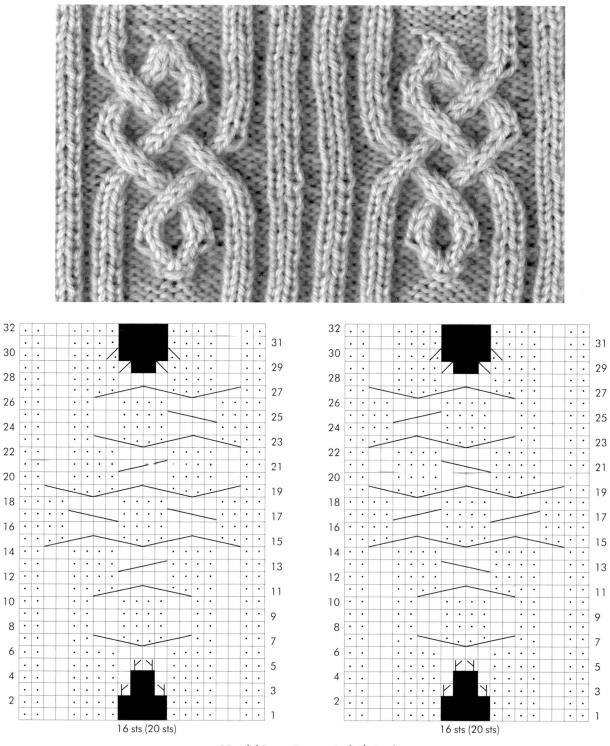

Vendel Loop Down Left & Right

herkja

Herkja is the perfect name for a garment in a book dealing with cross-cultural references. In the Icelandic Poetic Edda, *Herkja is described as being a former concubine to, and serving as a maid in the court of, Atli. Atli, in turn, supposedly alludes to Attila the Hun, and later in the book you will see several references to East European and Asian ornamentation.*

The pattern on Herkja is related to the Vendel pattern, discussed in Viking Patterns for Knitting, *and the pattern got its name from an area in Sweden where a huge number of artifacts have been found; so many, in fact, that Swedish historians refer to the period just prior to the Viking age as the Vendel era.*

Sizes   XS/S (ML, 1–2 X, 3–4 X)

Finished measurements

Chest   37 (42½, 48, 53½) in
         94 (108, 122, 136) cm
Length   19¾ (21, 22, 23¼) in
         50 (53, 56, 59) cm

Materials
Yarn   Silky Wool XL (p. 14)
Yarn amounts 550 (650, 750, 850) g
Needles   US size 8 / 5 mm
                  2 dpn US size 8 / 5 mm for I-cord
                  Cable needle

Gauge   17 sts × 24 rows in stockinette or block
             pattern = 4 × 4 in / 10 × 10 cm
1 block, 8 rows = slightly less than 1¼ in / 3 cm high.
Adjust needle size to obtain correct gauge if necessary.

Edge Stitches The outermost st at each side is an edge st. Edge sts are included in the stitch counts and are always knitted unless otherwise specified.

Note Each block consists of 6 sts and 8 rows. The pattern alternates between stockinette and reverse stockinette blocks. Make sure that a stockinette block meets a reverse stockinette block at the side. The garment can easily be lengthened in increments of 1 repeat of the cable panel, 4 blocks in length, approx 4¾ in / 12 cm.

Charts Vendel Loop Up Left and Right, p. 32.

Block pattern (multiple of 12+6 sts)
Rows 1, 3, 5, 7: *K6, p6; repeat from * and end with k6
Rows 2, 4, 6, 8: * P6, k6; repeat from * and end with p6
Rows 9, 11, 13, 15: * P6, k6; repeat from * and end with p6
Rows 10, 12, 14, 16: * K6, p6; repeat from * and end with k6
Repeat these 16 rows.

Back
Cast on 80 (92, 104, 116) sts and work in block pattern inside edge sts, beginning on Row 2, WS. When there are 9 (9, 10, 10) blocks in length, the piece should measure 11¾ (13, 13, 14¼) in / 30 (33, 33, 36) cm. Now shape armholes by binding off 6 sts at each side = 68 (80, 92, 104) sts. Work 6 (7, 7, 8) more blocks. The armhole should now measure 8 (9, 9, 10¼) in / 20 (23, 23, 26) cm. Using a separate strand for each, bind off 25 (31, 37, 43) sts for each shoulder and the center 18 sts for back neck.

Left Front
Cast on 58 (64, 70, 76) sts and work in pattern as follows, beginning on WS: Edge st, p2 (stockinette rib), work 16 sts of last row of cable panel following the chart Vendel Loop Up Right, p2 (stockinette rib), 36 (42, 48, 54) sts in block pattern, edge st. Continue as set until same length as back to armhole. Bind off 6 sts at the side for the armhole. *At the same time*, begin decreasing inside the panel at front

edge to shape neckline: work until 1 st before the first stockinette rib, k2tog (1ˢᵗ st of rib together with last st of block pattern so that the rib continues unbroken); complete row. Decrease the same way on every 8ᵗʰ row 6 times total. When armhole is same length as on back, bind off 25 (31, 37, 43) sts for shoulder. Now the 21 sts of front edge remain. Cast on a new edge st at the shoulder and continue in cable pattern for 3½ in / 9 cm. Bind off.

Right Front

Work as for left front, reversing shaping and following chart Vendel Loop Up Left. The first row is worked as: Edge st, 36 (42, 48, 54) sts block pattern, p2 (stockinette rib), 16 sts cable panel, p2, edge st. Work the decreases for the front neck as ssk, joining the last st of the stockinette rib with 1ˢᵗ st of block.

Sleeve Cuffs

Make one cuff following chart Vendel Loop Up Right and the other following chart Vendel Loop Up Left. Cast on 22 sts and set up pattern: Edge st, p2 (stockinette rib), 16 sts of last row of Vendel Loop cable panel, p2 (stockinette rib), edge st. Work 2 pattern repeats and then bind off.

Sleeves

Pick up and knit 48 sts along one long side of cuff (pick up 3 sts for every 4 rows) and cast on an edge st at each side = 50 sts. Work in block pattern beginning on Row 2 (WS). There should be 8 complete repeats inside the edge sts but the sleeves *are not* symmetrical. Increase 1 st at each side on every 8ᵗʰ row 8 (0, 0, 0) times, on every 4ᵗʰ row 4 (18, 18, 11) times, and then on every other row 0 (0, 0, 10) times = 74 (86, 86, 92) sts. When the sleeve is 10 (10, 9, 9) blocks in length and measures approx 11¾ (11¾, 13, 13) in / 30 (30, 33, 33) cm above cuff, place marker at each side and then work 8 more rows (1 complete block). Bind off. Work the other sleeve the same way, *reversing patterning so the sleeves are mirror-image.*

Finishing

Block pieces. Undo bound-off sts and join shoulders with three-needle bind-off. Seam front bands at center back neck and sew band down along back neck. Attach sleeves, making sure that the block patterns match. Seam sides and sleeves. *Tie:* For each tie, with dpn, pick up and knit 3 sts where you like along front edge and make an I-cord 11¾ in / 30 cm long, p. 185.

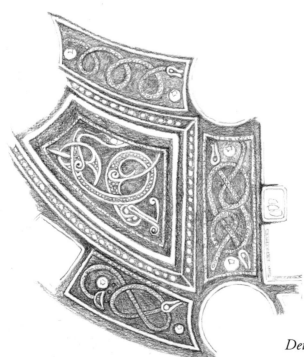

Detail from the Hunterston Brooch, Hunterston, Scotland

In *Viking Patterns for Knitting* I analyze what I have named the Lillbjärs panel in its basic shape with variations. I have since found other variations of this very attractive pattern. Here's a version where the loops have been mirrored and staggered. Among the objects in the Scottish St. Ninian's Isle treasure is a silver bowl with this very pattern, (not shown) and more examples can be found in the Book of Kells, which is a real gold mine for an interlace designs

explorer like myself. Another wonderful Scottish artifact is The Hunterston Brooch, with one repeat on each side of the central motif (shown on the previous page).

It is entirely possible to repeat just the upper or lower half to create a less dense version of the initial Lillbjärs panel. For this panel, the same chart can be used for a mirrored version—you simply start on row 25 and then continue repeating all the rows of the chart.

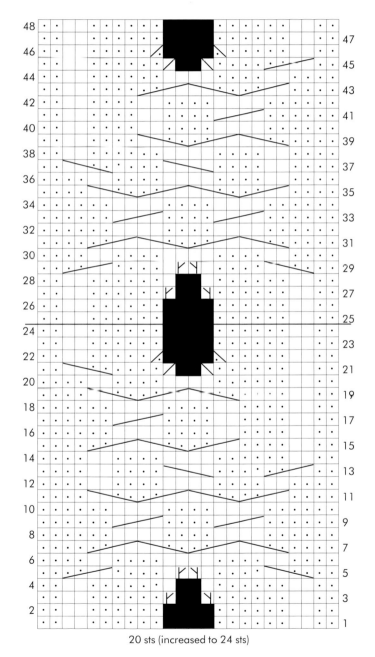

20 sts (increased to 24 sts)

Lillbjärs Staggered

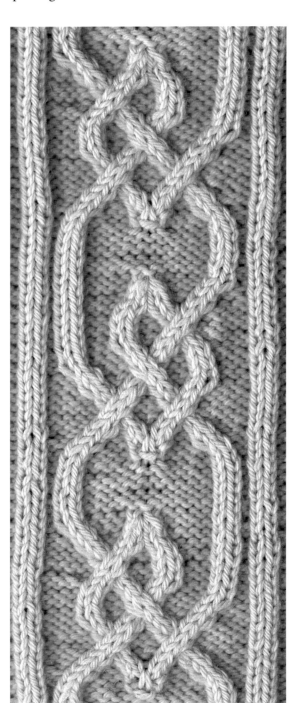

Here is the Lillbjärs pattern developed one step further by mirroring the loops in all four directions. This is a pattern favored in Islamic art as well as by the Langobards. The below beautiful stone fragment from Italy really shows the pattern's decorative potential.

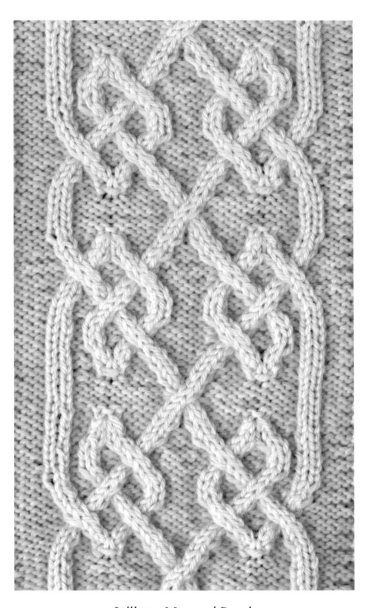

*Langobardic stone fragment, on display in the
Santa Giulia Museo, Brescia, Italy*

Lillbjärs Mirrored Panel

Detail from the Ardagh chalice, found in Ardagh, County Limerick, Ireland

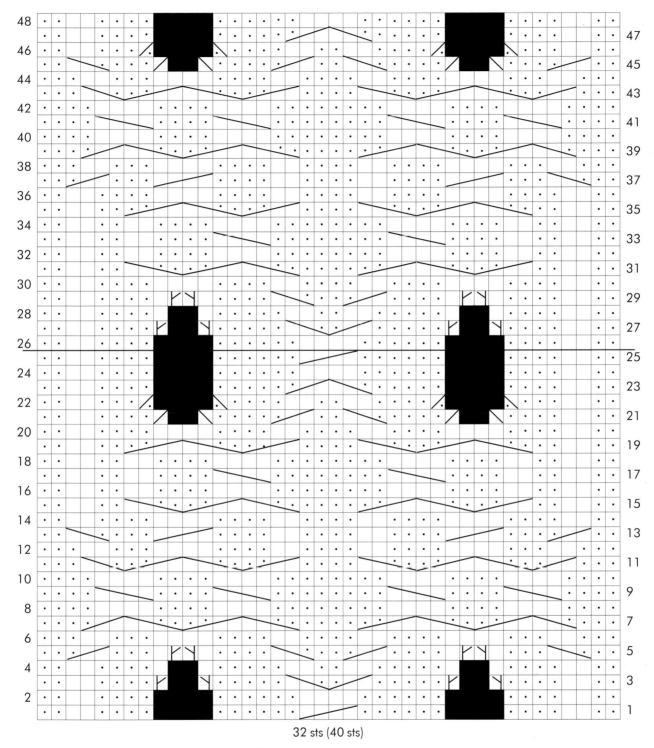

32 sts (40 sts)

Lillbjärs Mirrored Panel

OSK

Ósk is an Icelandic word that translates into "request" or "wish". Consequently, I thought Osk would be a good name for a garment that is truly to wish for. The unusual shape will enhance any figure. You can close it with ties or with a pretty pin. And it is not even all that difficult to knit. What more could you ask for? If I wasn't pretty handy with needles myself, I would have asked someone to make one for me.

The Lillbjärs Staggered pattern is another design with roots in Viking Patterns for Knitting, *but with a different twist (if you pardon the pun); a good example of the developmental potential of Viking Knits.*

Sizes   S (M, L, XL, XXL, XXXL)

Finished measurements

Chest	37 (39½, 43¼, 46½, 49¾, 52¾) in
	94 (100, 110, 118, 126, 134) cm
Length	29½ (30, 30¼, 30¾, 31, 31½) in
	75 (76, 77, 78, 79, 80) cm

Materials
Yarn   Silky Wool XL (p. 14)
Yarn amounts   500 (550, 600, 650, 700, 750) g
Needles   US size 8 / 5 mm

Gauge   17 sts × 24 rows in stockinette or moss st = 4 × 4 in / 10 × 10 cm
Adjust needle size to obtain correct gauge if necessary.

Edge stitches The outermost st at each side is an edge st. Edge sts are included in the stitch counts and are always knitted unless otherwise specified.

Note Do not splice yarns at the front or armhole edges.

Chart Lillbjärs Staggered p. 37.

Moss Stitch
   Row 1: * K1, p1; repeat from *
   Rows 2 and 4: Knit over knit and purl over purl
   Row 3: * P1, k1; repeat from *
Repeat these 4 rows.

Back

Cast on 100 (104, 108, 112, 116, 120) sts and purl 1 row on WS. *Set up pattern on next, RS, row:* Edge st, k1, p1, work 45 (47, 49, 51, 53, 55) moss st, p1, k2, p1, work 45 (47, 49, 51, 53, 55) moss sts, p1, k1, edge st. Throughout, there will be a knit st inside the edge st at each side so that a 2-st knit rib will be formed when the garment is seamed. The next st in at each side is worked in reverse stockinette to form a border for the moss stitch. Likewise, 1 st in reverse stockinette separates the 2 knit sts at the center from the moss stitch sections.

Continue as set until piece measures 1¼ in / 3 cm. Now decrease at the sides and center on WS as follows: edge st, p1, ssk, work until 2 sts before the center 2 purl sts, k2tog, p2, ssk, work until 4 sts remain and end with k2tog, p1, edge st = 4 sts decreased across row. Work this decrease row on every 10th row 10 times total = 60 (64, 68, 72, 76, 80) sts remain. When piece measures 20½ in / 52 cm, place a marker at each side. Cast on 2 sts at each side = 64 (68, 72, 76, 80, 84) sts and work 3 stockinette sts inside the edge st at each side. This will form the edging for the armhole and roll towards the WS. There should also be 1 st in reverse stockinette inside the edge sts as before. Continue without further shaping. When armhole, as measured from marker, is 8¼ (8¾, 9, 9½, 9¾, 10¼) in / 21 (22, 23, 24, 25, 26) cm, shape shoulders with short rows, beginning at neck edge: Work until 9 (10, 11, 12, 13, 14) sts remain; turn and work back until 9 (10, 11, 12, 13, 14) sts remain. Turn and work the next 2 rows each 9 (10, 11, 12, 13, 14) sts shorter. Bind off remaining 28 sts for back neck. Using a separate strand

of yarn for each, bind off 16 (18, 20, 22, 24, 26) sts for each shoulder.

Side Gores

Cast on 31 (33, 37, 39, 43, 45) sts and purl 1 row on WS.
Set up pattern: Edge st, k1, p1, work 25 (27, 31, 33, 37, 39) moss sts, p1, k1, edge st.
There will be a knit rib inside the edge st at each side and a reverse stockinette st inside the knit rib.
When piece measures 1¼ in / 3 cm, begin decreasing at the sides of every 10th WS row: Edge st, p1, ssk, work until 4 sts remain and end with k2tog, p1, edge st. Decrease the same way a total of 10 times. When piece measures 20½ in / 52 cm, bind off all 11 (13, 17, 19, 23, 25) sts.

Left Front

Cast on 51 (53, 55, 57, 59, 61) sts and purl 1 row on WS.
Set up pattern: Edge st, k1, p1, work 21 (23, 25, 27, 29, 31) moss sts, p1, k2, k20 (garter st), k3, edge st (the front edge will be shaped and roll inwards as the armhole edges). After 6 rows, over the 20 garter sts, start working the panel, *beginning on Row 1 of chart.*
When piece measures 1¼ in / 3 cm, begin decreasing at the side as on the back on every 10th row 10 times = 41 (43, 45, 47, 49, 51) sts.
When piece measures 20½ in / 52 cm, place a marker at the side.
Cast on 2 sts at the side = 43 (45, 47, 49, 51, 53) sts, with 3 stockinette sts inside the edge st at the armhole as on back. Continue without further shaping. When armhole, as measured from marker, is 8¼ (8¾, 9, 9½, 9¾, 10¼) in / 21 (22, 23, 24, 25, 26) cm long, shape shoulders with short rows, beginning at front edge: Work until 9 (10, 11, 12, 13, 14) sts remain; turn and work back. Work the 27 sts of col-

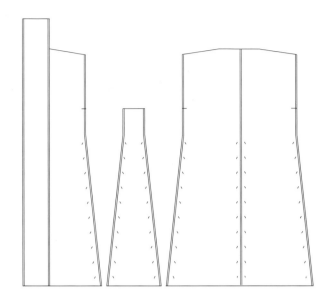

lar; turn and work back. Using a separate strand, bind off 16 (18, 20, 22, 24, 26) sts for shoulder. Continue over the 27 sts of collar for another 4 in / 10 cm. Bind off.

Right Front

Work as for left front but *begin the chart on Row 25* so the pattern will be mirror-image.
Cast on 51 (53, 55, 57, 59, 61) sts and purl 1 row on WS.
Set up pattern: Edge st, k3, work 20 sts following chart, work 21 (23, 25, 27, 29, 31) moss sts, p1, k1, edge st.

Finishing

Block pieces. Undo bound-off sts and join shoulders with three-needle bind-off. Sew or join the collar with three-needle bind-off at center back and then sew down along back neck. Attach gores to front and back below the armhole markers.

Box-shaped brooch with the Lillbjärs border, Gotland, Sweden

Rings & Chains

Join the ends of a band and you have created a ring. In many cultures, the closed ring symbolizes togetherness (e.g. the wedding ring in Western tradition) and/or eternity. The ring as a symbolic representation of the sun, and thus of life, is commonplace in many cultures.

Another common way of symbolically interpreting the ring is as Ouroboros, a serpent eating its own tail. Ouroboros appears in ancient Egyptian and Greek texts, and in Aztec imagery. In Norse mythology a corresponding creature, Jörmungandr, the Midgard Serpent, encircles the world. Ouroboros symbolizes wholeness, our entire being, eternity and the cyclical character of our existence.

Egyptian mythology also includes Shen, a ring with a tangent representing encirclement, which is what the Egyptian word actually means. Stretched-out versions of the Shen, Cartouches, encircle the names of Pharaohs and are commonly found carved into walls inside pyramids.

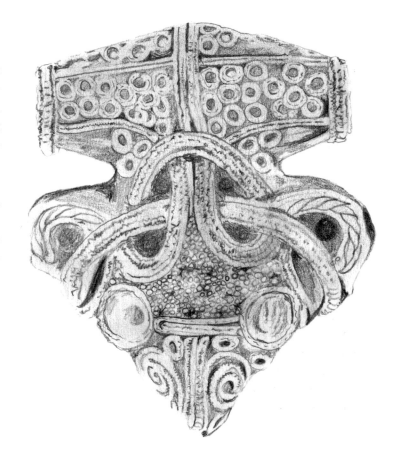

Thor's Hammer pendant, Sigtuna, Sweden

Egyptian Shen symbol

Indigenous North Americans often refer to "the hoop" that holds people together and represents the cyclic repetition of our existence. Another concept of Native American tradition is the Medicine Wheel, used to preserve the health of man and earth. To the Maoris of New Zealand, the ring can also symbolize the interplay between head, hand and heart.

A pendant from Sigtuna, Sweden shows a Viking age ring ornamentation: Filigree rings decorate Mjölner, the hammer of the god Thor. Basic individual rings like these were covered in my *Viking Patterns for Knitting* book, but they can naturally be varied in shape and size in a multitude of ways.

Here's a larger version of the ring; the bands can be moved outwards for as long as you like before you turn and let them work their way inwards again. This way you can create a ring of any desired size. The two rows between expansions and contractions are used to keep the pattern in line with other pattern elements, if present.

Two bands can be woven to form a cross inside the ring. This happens to be the symbol of Gungner, the sword of the Norse god Odin. Gungner was forged by dwarfs who gave it to Odin. It always hits its intended target, and always returns to Odin's hand.

Thus it's hard to imagine a better place to have such an ornament than on a sword like the depicted one from Lardal, Norway. In the shape of an animal, it has also been used on a box-shaped brooch from Gotland, Sweden. The Saxons provide an example from Bassingham, England, and the most exquisite example stems from a zoomorphic initial in a French 9th century Psalter: A complex braided border adorns the vertical line in the B, including, randomly as it may seem, a single Ring on a Cross.

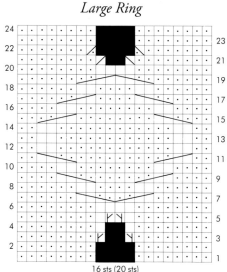

Large Ring

16 sts (20 sts)

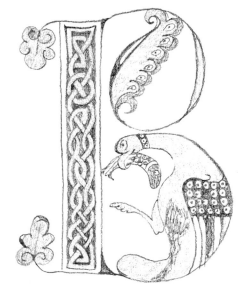

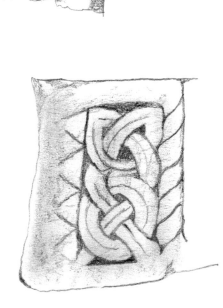

Above: Zoomorphic initial from 9th century Psalter, Tours, France
Top right: Iron age sword, Lardal, Norway
Right: Detail from a Saxon stone, Bassingham, Lincolnshire, England

A row of Ring Crosses decorate the below stirrup from Gotland, Sweden (side view). They can also be combined to form a beautiful border, seen here on the depicted hogback, a Viking age grave stone of a type only found on the British Isles and shaped like a Viking longhouse (bottom of page).

On the below cross shaft from Yorkshire, England, the same basic motif appears, but the bands run through two rings. The ornamentation also includes a Ring on Crossed Bands and S-hooks.

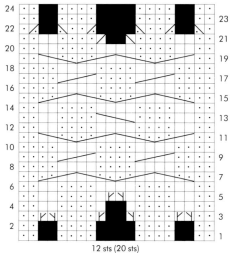

12 sts (20 sts)

Ring on Cross

Above left: Decor on stirrup, Gotland, Sweden
Above right: Section of a cross-shaft, Yorkshire, England
Left: Decor on box-shaped brooch, Gotland, Sweden
Below: Penrith hogback, 10th century, England

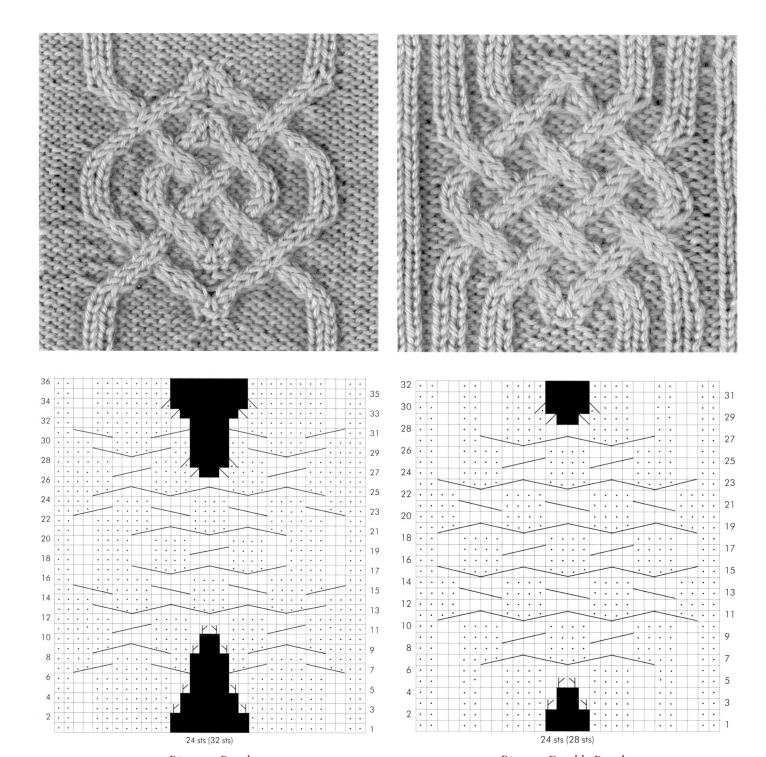

Rings on Bands

24 sts (32 sts)

Ring on Double Bands

24 sts (28 sts)

There are versions with four bands braided into a ring as on the sword hilt from Tipperary, Ireland. The sword is Viking age, and the style is referred to as Irish-Scandinavian. The same basic pattern, but in a totally different style, can be seen on a slab from Isle of Man with a Crucifixion motif.

Regardless of size, the ring may be elongated to any desired length. Thus, both the basic ring and the elongated variety can be sized e.g. to allow framing of other motifs. Swatch and chart below.

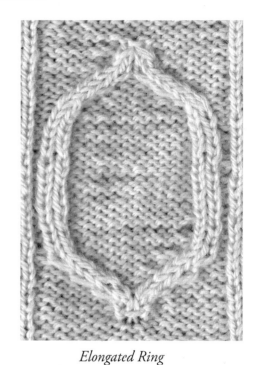

Above: Fragment of stone cross Kirk Andreas, Isle of Man, Great Britain
Below: Detail on 11ᵗʰ century sword, Tipperary, Ireland

Elongated Ring

16 sts (20 sts)

Chains

Linked together, rings form Chains. The shortest possible chain consists of two linked rings. The Mongolian Khalka people, who regard themselves as descendants of Genghis Khan, seem to be particularly fond of this pattern, referred to as Khan's Bracelet. One example can be seen below, decorating a saddle.

On Viking age objects I have only found a handful of examples of basic chains, but a ski from Laitila, Finland is one of them (next page). In the Chain Narrow, the aforementioned elongated rings are linked, while the Chain Wide links larger rings. For both patterns, the rings can be made longer and/or larger.

Lacquer chest inlay, Korea 1890–1910

Chain Narrow

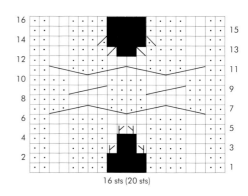

16 sts (20 sts)

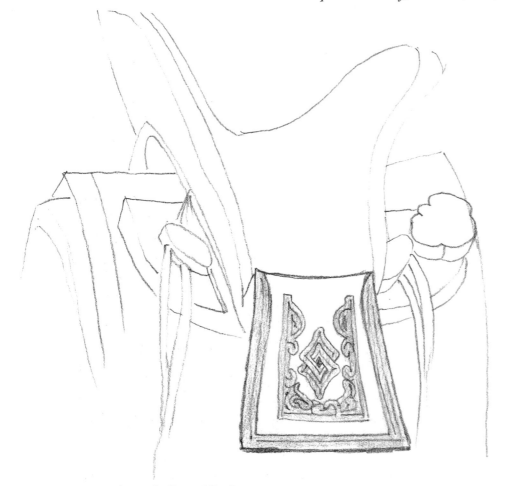

Mongolian Khalka saddle decoration

48

Chain Wide

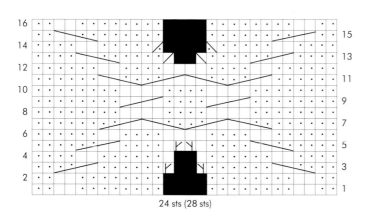

24 sts (28 sts)

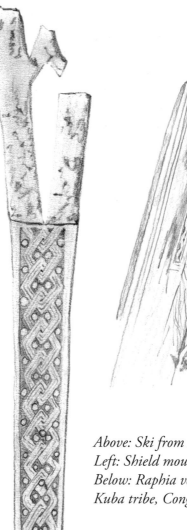

Above: Ski from Laitila, Finland
Left: Shield mount, Vendel, Sweden
Below: Raphia velvet embroidery,
Kuba tribe, Congo

Surface patterns can also be created by linking rings in all directions, and again the Congolese Kuba people appear in my research, this time with another embroidered fabric.

TOVA

As it happens the Swedish word "tova" is both a name with roots way back in Norse prehistory, and a verb. The name is a short form of names related to Thor, the Norse God of Thunder. In Swedish the verb means to felt or full. The beret may not be a candidate for felting, but the bag certainly is!

The beret shape will frame the face and with the matching bag this set is a very versatile complement to any outfit. And in combining a basic Viking Knits pattern, a narrow chain, with a more spectacular one, the Little Knot and Fourknot, it spans a, small but still, corner of the Knitting Universe.

Size Woman's

Finished measurements

Head circumference	21¾–22¾ in
	55–58 cm
Bag approx	11¾ × 6 × 11¾ in
	30 × 15 × 30 cm

Materials

Yarn (p. 14)

Beret	Silky Wool XL 100 g
Bag	Silky Wool XL 200 g

Notions A piece of thin, hard foam, approx 6 × 11¾ in / 15 × 30 cm (size piece to fit the bottom of your bag). Lining fabric, approx 17¾ × 27½ in / 45 × 70 cm.

Needles

Beret US size 6 / 4 mm
16 in / 40 cm circular US size 7 / 4.5 mm
Set of 4 or 5 dpn US size 7 / 4.5 mm for crown shaping
Bag US size 7 / 4.5 mm
16 in / 40 cm circular US size 7 / 4.5 mm
Set of 4 or 5 dpn US size 7 / 4.5 mm
Cable needle

Gauge 18 sts × 26 rows in stockinette on larger needles = 4 × 4 in / 10 × 10 cm
Adjust needle sizes to obtain correct gauge if necessary.

Edge Stitches The outermost st at each side is an edge st. Edge sts are included in the stitch counts and are always knitted unless otherwise specified.

Charts Chain Narrow, p. 48, Little Knot & Fourknot, p. 91.

Beret

Brim: With smaller needles, cast on 23 sts and set up pattern as follows, beginning on RS: Edge st, k3 (stockinette), work 16 sts cable pattern following Chain Narrow chart, k2 (stockinette), edge st. Work 8 pattern repeats and then bind off rather tightly. Seam the short ends of the brim as invisibly as possible, making sure that the seam doesn't pucker.

Crown: With larger size circular, along the edge that *doesn't* have the extra stockinette st inside the edge st, pick up and knit 1 st in every row = 132 sts. Join and place marker for beginning of round. Knit around in stockinette for 4 in / 10 cm.

Place markers to divide the cap into 6 sections of 22 sts each.

Crown shaping: Beginning at first marker (beginning of round), *k2tog, knit until 2 sts before next marker, ssk, slip marker*. Repeat from * to * around. Decrease the same way on every other round until 12 sts remain. Change to dpn when sts no longer fit around circular. Cut yarn and draw end through remaining sts.

Bag

Bottom: With US 7 / 4.5 mm circular, cast on 44 sts and work back and forth in garter st until there are 20 knit ridges.

Front: Work 12 rows in reverse stockinette with 1 stockinette st inside the edge st at each side. Next, work the Little Knot with Fourknot centered on the piece. After completing charted rows, work another 8 rows as set before cable motif. Set piece aside.

Back: With US 7 / 4.5 mm circular and RS facing, pick up and knit 44 sts along cast-on edge, and work back as for front.

Sides: With US 7 / 4.5 mm circular, pick up and knit 1 st in each knit ridge along one side = 20 sts. Work in cable pattern following the Chain Narrow chart, with 1 stockinette st inside the edge st at each side. Work 4 pattern repeats. Set piece aside and work the other side the same way. All four sides should now be the same length.

Handles: With US 7 / 4.5 mm circular, pick up and knit the sts for all of the sections, eliminating all the edge sts with ssk before each intersection and k2tog after = 120 sts. Join and continue in stockinette for 3 rounds. Next, beginning between the back and one side: work the side sts, k8, work the next 24 sts (center of front) with waste yarn; place sts back on left needle and knit again with working yarn. Knit the last 8 sts and then repeat on the other side and back.

Knit around in stockinette for 2½ in / 6 cm and then bind off. Carefully remove the waste yarn, and, with dpn, pick up and knit the released sts and 2 sts at each side (or short end) for the handle. Bind off.

Finishing

Sew the four seams.

If you want pieces that will be extra soft, dense, and stable, full the cap and bag. Place the garments in a nylon net washing bag (stuff with a hand towel to facilitate the fulling) and wash with a half or full load at 104°F / 40°C. Shape pieces and let dry.

Cut out the base for the bag and attach with a few stitches at each corner. Make the lining slightly larger than the bag and sew in along the bag's first row of stockinette.

The beret knitted in Favorite Wool

Stamp, Gudme, Denmark

Twisted Rings

Twisted once, rings turn into the symbol of Eternity, or a horizontal Figure Eight if you will. This pattern is abundant on Viking age objects. For a pleasing knitted result, you really have no option but to knit it like a regular, vertical Figure Eight.

To make the smallest and most basic Figure Eight, knit following the Twist chart on page 150. The charted repeat can of course be knitted over and over to make a Twist pattern. Shown here on the left is a larger version.

The gold bead from Gram, Denmark, displays an Eternity symbol next to a loop (see the drawing on p. 16), while it's combined with a Little Knot on the stamp from Gudme, Denmark. To me, the *Guldgubbe* (literally "golden geezer", a gold foil figure) is one of the most endearing examples of uses of the Eternity symbol. These Guldgubbar, predating the Viking age, have been found in the thousands in Scandinavia, but this atypical specimen was discovered in Bornholm, Denmark, and belongs to a small group of similar *Bird Men*. The Bird Men are male figures in poses indicating flight, and recent archaeological research has theorized about a possible connection to shamanic journeys.

Outside of the Viking world, I have spotted the Figure Eight on e.g. a 19th century Menominee Indian bag decorated with thunderbirds. The drawing of a carved bone pendant shows what New Zealand Maoris refer to as a *pikorua* or *rauiri*. It is believed to symbolize how two persons meet, and while life may separate them, they are always brought back together.

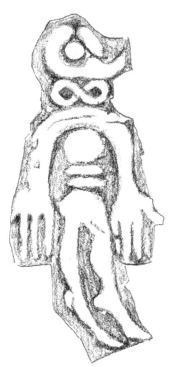

Bird Man, Guldgubbe,
Bornholm, Denmark

Maori Pikorua,
New Zealand

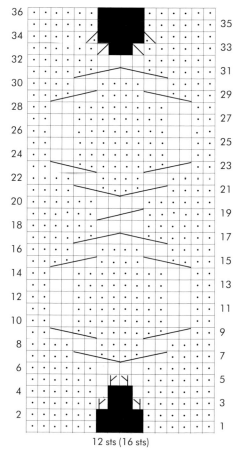

12 sts (16 sts)

Twisted Ring / Large Figure Eight

The basic Figure Eight is symmetrical, but by using different combinations of beginnings and endings variations can be made, as seen in the below swatches.

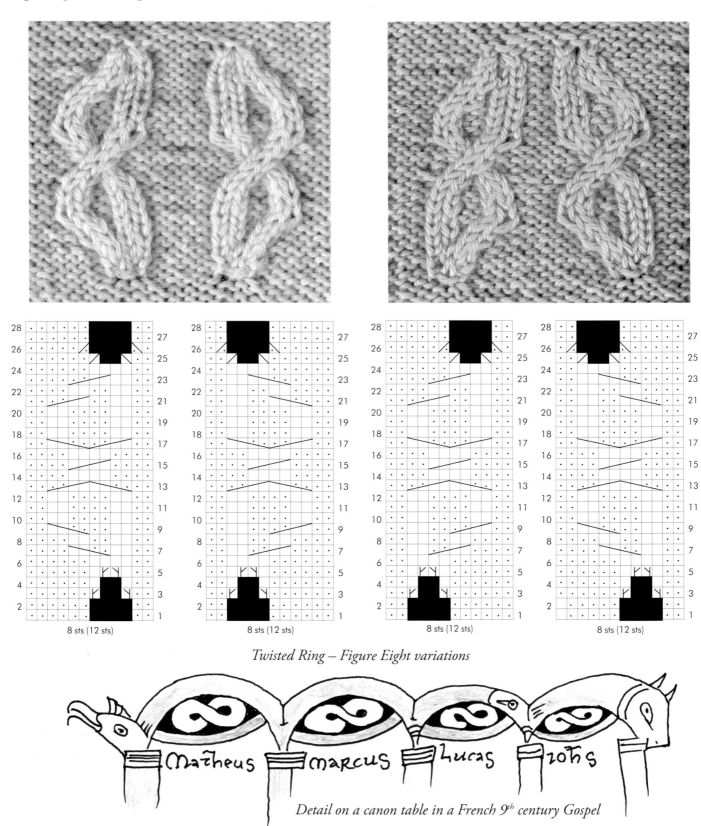

Twisted Ring – Figure Eight variations

Detail on a canon table in a French 9ᵗʰ century Gospel

Just as you can weave a band through a ring, you can weave it through a Figure Eight. The Vikings, however, didn't make much use of this pattern, leading me to believe for some time that it was my own invention. This was until I identified it on the abundantly ornamented mount from Solberga, Sweden, where it appears along with Twists, Overhand Knots, Trefoils, Elongated Trefoils, Twisted Wing Loops… to name a few. The Figure Eight on Band makes another appearance framing the Gospel according to John on one of the pages of The Egmont Gospels, a medieval illuminated manuscript from England (not shown).

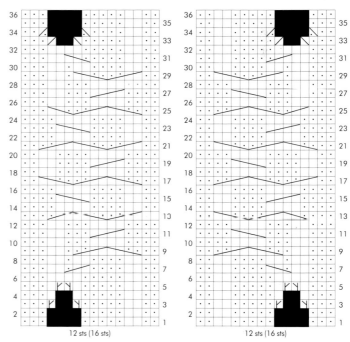

Figure Eight on Band, Left and Right

Later, in a French illuminated manuscript from the 9th century, I discovered the twin version, where two mirrored Eights are placed side by side with a pair of crossing bands twined through them (see next spread).

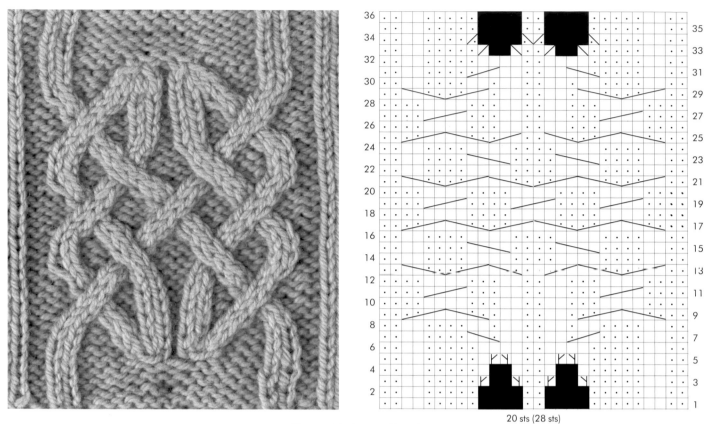

Figure Eights on Bands

Detail on a canon table from The Gospels of St Cyr of Nevers, f 23v, 9th century, France

signild

Some claim that the name Signild means beloved, others that it means victorious. I don't have a strong opinion, but what I do know is that Signild the cardigan has been with me for a long time. Among my earliest Viking Knits designs, she has had many incarnations and is still a wardrobe staple.

Adorned with the very pretty Figure Eight on Bands pattern and made in the lovely Silky Wool XL yarn, this version is one of my absolute favorites, even though I'm not supposed to favor any one of my own designs. Will she become one of your favorites as well?

Sizes   S (M, L, XL, XXL)

Finished measurements
Chest   38¾ (41¼, 44¼, 46¾, 48¼) in
               98 (104, 112, 118, 122) cm
Length   19¼ (19¼, 20½, 20½, 20½) in
               49 (49, 52, 52, 52) cm

Materials
Yarn   Silky Wool XL (p. 14)
Yarn amounts 500 (550, 600, 650, 700) g
Notions   5 buttons, ⅝–¾ in / 18–20 mm
Needles   US sizes 7 and 8 / 4.5 and 5 mm

Gauge   17 sts × 24 rows in stockinette on larger
                  needles = 4 × 4 in / 10 × 10 cm
Adjust needle sizes to obtain correct gauge if necessary.

Edge Stitches The outermost st at each side is an edge st. Edge sts are included in the stitch counts and are always knitted, even along front edges.

Note Make sure that the ribbing always has a knit st inside the edge st on RS and a knit st next to the panel.

Charts Figure Eights on Bands, p. 56, and connecting chart A, p. 58. The two smallest sizes are worked following Rows 3–34 and the three largest sizes Rows 1–36. If necessary, work the rows at the end with knit over knit and purl over purl.

Back

With smaller needles, cast on 83 (89, 95, 101, 107) sts and work 5 rows in ribbing as follows: begin on WS with (k1, p1) 7 (8, 9, 10, 11) times = 14 (16, 18, 20, 22) sts ribbing, 19 sts of the main chart following Row R2, 17 (19, 21, 23, 25) sts in p1, k1 ribbing, 19 sts panel and (p1, k1) 7 (8, 9, 10, 11) times = 14 (16, 18, 20, 22) sts ribbing.

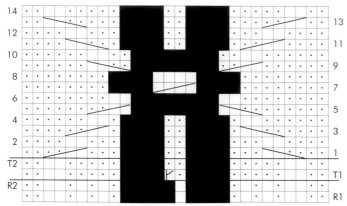

19 sts rib increased to 20 sts cable panel

Chart A

Change to larger needles and work in stockinette over the ribbing. Work the first 2 rows, T1, of the panel (note the increases) and T2 = 85 (91, 97, 103, 109) sts, and then * Rows 1–14 following chart A. Next, work Rows 3–34 for two smallest sizes / Rows 1–36 for 3 larger sizes following the main chart. Repeat from * and end with Rows 1–14 of chart A.

When piece is 10¾ (10¼, 11, 10¾, 10¼) in / 27 (26, 28, 27, 26) cm long, shape armhole at each side. Bind off 1 st at each side and then decrease 1 st at each side on every other row 7 (8, 9, 10, 11) times = 69 (73, 77, 81, 85) sts. When armhole measures 8¼ (9¾, 9, 9½, 9¾) in / 21 (22, 23, 24, 25) cm, bind off the center 17 (19, 19, 21, 21) sts and work each side separately. Shape neck and shoulder with short rows, beginning at neck edge: Bind off 2 sts, work until 8 (8, 9, 9, 10) sts remain; turn and work back. Work 8 (8, 9, 9, 10) sts; turn and work back. Bind off remaining 24 (25, 27, 28, 30) sts for shoulder. Work the other side the same way, reversing shaping.

Left Front

With smaller needles, cast on 45 (49, 53, 57, 61) sts and work 5 rows in ribbing as follows: begin on WS with (k1, p1) 6 (7, 8, 9, 10) times = 12 (14, 16, 18, 20) sts ribbing, 19 sts of the main chart following Row R2, and (p1, k1) 7 (8, 9, 10, 11) times = 14 (16, 18, 20, 22) sts ribbing. Change to larger needles and work in stockinette over the ribbing *except* for the 8 sts at front edge which continue in ribbing. Work the first 2 rows, T1, of the panel (note the increases) and T2 = 44 (48, 52, 56, 60) sts, and then * Rows 1–14 following chart A. Next, work Rows 3–34 / 1–36 following

the main chart. Repeat from * and end with Rows 1–14 of chart A.

When piece is 10¾ (10¼, 11, 10¾, 10¼) in / 27 (26, 28, 27, 26) cm long, shape armhole at each side as for back. *At the same time*, shape neck: ssk inside the 8 sts at front edge on every 4th row 6 (8, 9, 10, 11) times.

When armhole measures 8¼ (9¾, 9, 9½, 9¾) in / 21 (22, 23, 24, 25) cm, shape shoulder with short rows, beginning at neck edge: Work until 8 (8, 9, 9, 10) sts remain; turn and work back. Work 8 sts at front edge + 8 (8, 9, 9, 10) sts; turn and work back. With a separate strand of yarn, bind off 24 (25, 27, 28, 30) sts for shoulder.

Now 8 sts remain. Cast on a new edge st at the shoulder and work the 9 sts of front edge in k1, p1 ribbing as set until strip reaches center back neck. Bind off. Mark the spacing for 5 buttons spaced equally down front band, with the top one an inch or so / 2–3 cm below beginning of V-neck and the lowest immediately above the 5 rows of ribbing at bottom edge.

Right Front

Work as for Left Front, reversing shaping and with buttonholes spaced as for buttons. For each buttonhole, bind off 2 sts inside the 3 sts of front edge and, on the next row, cast on 2 sts over the gap. Shape neck with k2tog inside the 8 sts of front band.

Sleeves

With smaller needles, cast on 35 (37, 37, 39, 39) sts and work 5 rows in k1, p1 ribbing, beginning on WS. Change to larger needles and stockinette. Shape sleeve by increasing 1 st at each side on every 6th row 12 (12, 14, 14, 14) times and then on every 4th row 0 (0, 0, 1, 2) times = 59 (61, 65, 69, 71) sts. When sleeve is 16 in / 42 cm long, shape sleeve cap by first binding off 1 st at each side. Next, decrease 1 st at each side on every other row 7 (8, 9, 10, 11) times. Bind off 3 sts at the beginning of every row 10 times and then bind off remaining 13 (13, 15, 17, 17) sts.

Finishing

Block pieces. Undo bound-off sts and join shoulders with three-needle bind-off. Seam the short ends of bands at center back neck and sew band along back neck. Sew side and sleeve seams. Attach sleeves. Sew on buttons.

Figure Eight & Ring swatch

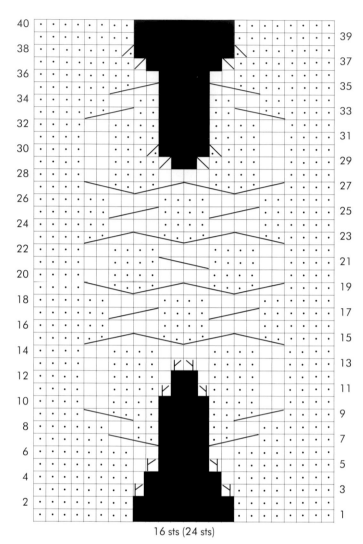

16 sts (24 sts)

Figure Eight & Ring chart

On the bead from Tissø, Denmark, as well as on the box-shaped brooch from Gotland, Sweden, a ring has been woven into the Eternity symbol; a pattern I interpret as signifying "Double Eternity". In a horizontal version, the same pattern decorates a Thor's hammer from Ödeshög,

Sweden, shown on the next page. This is basically the same pattern as a Ring on Bands, but the bands join to form a Large Figure Eight.

Above: Bead from Tissø, Denmark
Left: Brooch from Gotland, Sweden

The same motif, and one that resembles it but is in fact two Figure Eights intertwined, appears growing out of a circle periphery on a stone from Papil, Shetland, with a pair of Triquetras completing the ornamentation.

The same basic design can also be found on a stone from Bressay, Scotland, but with a less common motif, unfortunately impossible to make a knitted version of, placed between the Figure Eights. The "Q" initial, from a 10th century Homiliarium (a collection of commentaries to scriptures) from the Abbey of Saint Gall, Switzerland, uses the same motif.

Thor's Hammer pendant, Ödeshög, Sweden

Initial from Homiliarium, Swizerland

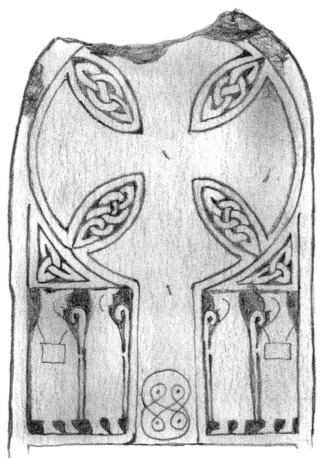

Stone from Papil, Shetland

Stone from Bressay, Scotland

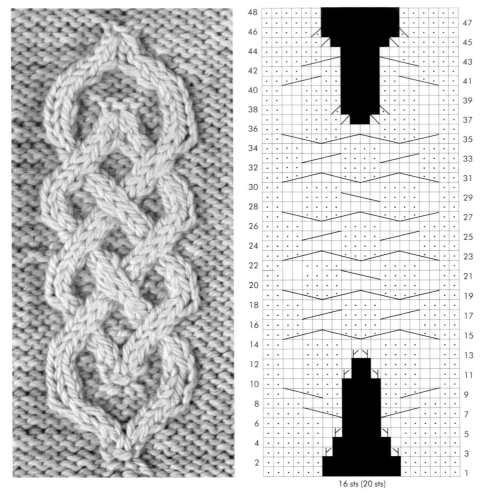

48
46
44
42
40
38
36
34
32
30
28
26
24
22
20
18
16
14
12
10
8
6
4
2

47
45
43
41
39
37
35
33
31
29
27
25
23
21
19
17
15
13
11
9
7
5
3
1

16 sts (20 sts)

Braided Figure Eights

Looped Rings

A ring can be twisted in a number of different ways, thus creating loops emerging from the ring. Positioning the twists at equal distances will create a Twist pattern (see p. 150) that can be made just as long as you want.

Twisting the ring twice with the "mother ring" larger than the "daughters" will create a ring motif with two loops flanking; a Looped Ring. In my research, I have found no examples of the basic form seen in the swatches, but in the depicted 10th century Gospel manuscript the Looped Ring is twined with two bands going straight through (above).

More commonly, the Looped Ring is combined with crossed bands. Instances can be seen on the Viking helmet fragment (eye and nose protection pieces, below left) from Gotland, Sweden, and in the square motif on an Irish High Cross of uncertain origin (below). Another swatch and chart shows the Looped Ring on a Cross with the bands cut (next page).

Viking helmet fragment with Looped Rings, Gotland, Sweden

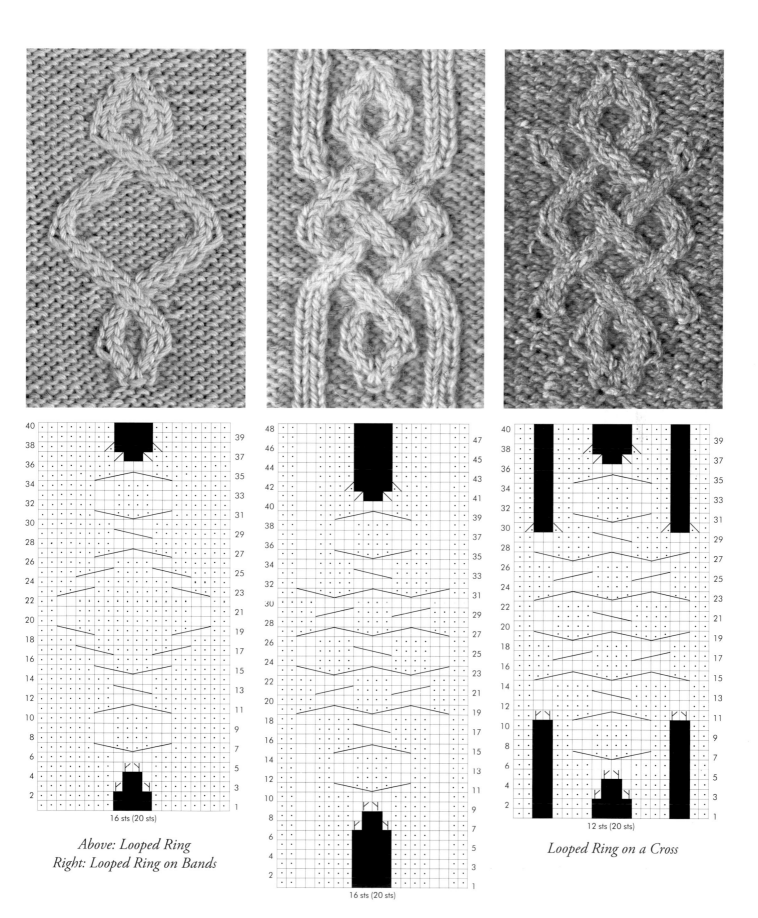

Above: Looped Ring
Right: Looped Ring on Bands

16 sts (20 sts)

16 sts (20 sts)

Looped Ring on a Cross

12 sts (20 sts)

These patterns can be combined in various ways. On the Northern Germanic buckle from 8th or 9th century Tromsø, Norway, the Eternity symbol and the Looped Ring are intertwined in the most beautiful way. A bead-separator, used to hold rows of beads in parallel in Viking necklaces, from Bornholm, Denmark, displays a similar ornamentation, and on the intriguing picture stone from Gotland, Sweden, the Figure Eight and the Looped Ring are combined into a continuous loop to produce a visually similar effect.

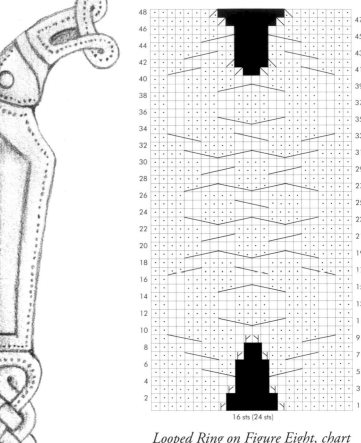

Looped Ring on Figure Eight, chart

16 sts (24 sts)

Above left: Bead-separator, Denmark
Left: Picture stone from Ardre, Gotland, Sweden
Below: Buckle, Tromsø, Norway

Looped Ring on Figure Eight, swatch

Looped Rings, joined as in the sketch, have been on my "find-examples-list" for years. For a long time, the best I could come up with was an ornament in a 15th century Ethiopian manuscript, where the links have loops at just one end and are linked at every other crossing like a regular chain. Later, I found a similar version on the Gaut's Cross from the Isle of Man. The Congolese Bushongo tribe finally provided an exact sample in the pattern of a striped fabric. Even with the few "real world" examples, I believe this beautiful border deserves a place in the book, or two, actually, since I liked it so much that I made a wide and a narrow version (next page).

Below left: Detail of border on a picture stone, Tjängvide, Gotland, Sweden
Below middle: Detail on Gaut's Cross, Isle of Man, Great Britain
Below right: From an Ethiopian manuscript

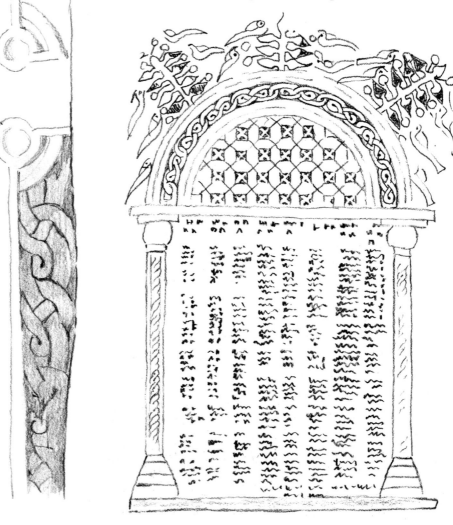

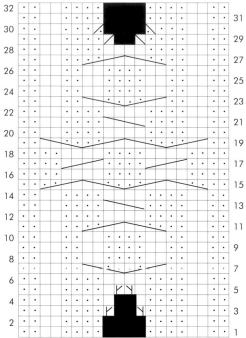

Above: Bushongo textile, Congo
Left: Looped Ring Chain Narrow
Below: Looped Ring Chain Wide

16 sts (20 sts)

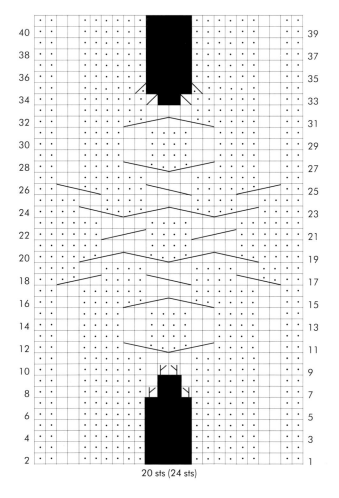

20 sts (24 sts)

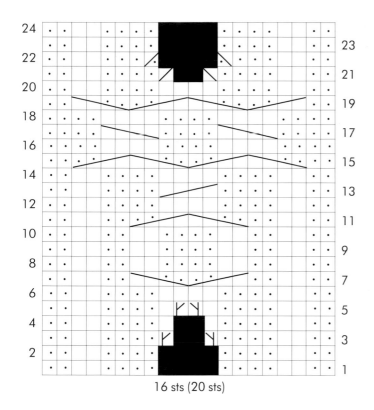

Looped Ring Chain & Chain

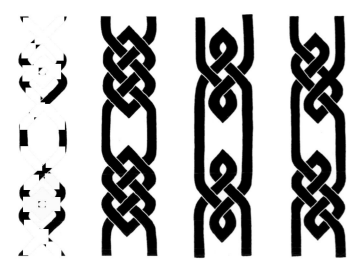

Visually, Looped Rings can be connected in many ways. In the first example, far left, the small loops are connected. In the next, the links have moved closer together and the loops are braided into the link. For both of these versions there are plenty of artifacts. The next is moving the link one more step inwards, as in the third border. For this version, artifacts are very scarce. Why is it that version one and two are frequent but version three unusual? Especially considering that this is not the case with version four, in which the loops are asymmetrically connected. Not necessarily the next logical step, but although artifacts may not be abundant, they are definitely not scarce. The unexpectedness of the human creative mind is intriguing.

FULLA

It's not often that I make skirts, and shrugs are even more rare in my "catalogue", but such a combo was an ideal candidate for this very distinct combination of cables and placed motifs—made in Silky Wool it's perfect for those days when it's neither hot nor cool.

When I chose this name for a Viking Knits design, I had the old Norse meaning in mind, where the name Fulla stands for fullness, completion. Fulla was the goddess Frigg's hand-maiden in whom Frigg would confide all her secrets. I had no idea at the time that Fulla is also a name used for an Arab world equivalent of Barbie! In a book full of hints about how Vikings might have influenced the Islamic culture and vice versa, how cool is that?

Sizes   SM (LXL)

Finished measurements
Skirt width at hips	39½ (47¼) in / 100 (120) cm
Length	24 in / 61 cm
Shrug	33 (34¼) in / 84 (87) cm including cuffs; 11¾–13¾ in / 30–35 cm wide

Materials
Yarn   Silky Wool (p. 14)
Yarn amounts
Skirt	350 (450) g
Shrug	150 (200) g
Notions	Round elastic 2–5 times personal waist or hip measurement
Needles	US sizes 4 and 6 / 3.5 and 4 mm 1 set of 5 dpn US size 2–3 / 3 mm for shrug cuffs Cable needle

Gauge   22 sts × 30 rows in stockinette on larger needles = 4 × 4 in / 10 × 10 cm
Adjust needle sizes to obtain correct gauge if necessary.

Edge stitches The outermost st at each side is an edge st. Edge sts are included in the stitch counts and are always knitted unless otherwise specified.

Note It is easy to lengthen or shorten the skirt. For a shorter skirt, space the increase rows more closely together and, for a longer skirt, space them further apart.

Charts Looped Ring Chain Narrow, p. 66 and Looped Ring on Cross motif, p. 63.

Skirt, back
With smaller needles, cast on 74 (86) sts and work in k2, p2 ribbing for 7 rows, beginning on WS with edge st, p1, k2 and ending with p1, edge st. When the sides are seamed, the knit sts at each side on RS will be joined into a 2-st rib. Change to larger needles and begin increasing immediately: Work 6 sts in ribbing, * RLI, p2, LLI, work 10 sts ribbing; repeat from * 5 (6) more times, ending the last repeat with 6 sts ribbing instead of 10. The increased sts should be worked in reverse stockinette to form the center of the pattern panels. Repeat this increase row every 6th row —there will be 2 more sts between the increases each time. *At the same time* as the last increase (there are now 8 sts of reverse stockinette), work the Looped Ring Chain Narrow beginning on Row 5 of the chart. There will be a 2-st rib outside and between each cable panel.
Complete the charted motif (Rows 6–32) and then work Rows 1–32. There are now 2 complete pattern repeats and the piece should measure 9½ in / 24 cm.
Now work knit over knit and purl over purl and begin increasing as follows: *Work 6 sts, RLI, 8 sts, LLI, work the

last 6 sts; repeat from *. Repeat this increase row on every 8th row (there will be 2 more stitches between ribs each time) to the garter st edging at bottom of skirt. When skirt is 17¾ in / 45 cm long (6 in / 15 cm shorter than total length), work Looped Ring on Cross motifs centered on each gore. When skirt is 23¾ in / 60 cm long, end with 7 rows, working in garter st between the ribs. Bind off knitwise on RS.

Skirt, front

Work the front as for the back.

Finishing

Block pieces. Seam sides, using mattress stitch for best results. Working through every other row at the top of the skirt, weave in 2–5 rows of round elastic.

Shrug

With US size 6 / 4 mm needles, cast on 92 sts (for both sizes) and purl 1 row = WS.

Set up pattern, RS: K2, * work 16 sts of Looped Ring Chain Narrow, k2, repeat from * 4 more times (the first and last sts are edge sts).

Work chart for Looped Ring Chain Narrow: first Rows 1–2 are worked 1 (3) times and then Rows 1–32 6 times. The piece should now measure 25¼ (26) in / 64 (66) cm. End with Rows 1–2 worked 0 (2) times.

Cuffs: Change to dpn and join to work in the round. Knit 1 round, binding off edge sts and decreasing (increasing) 1 st at the beginning and end of the 8 reverse stockinette sts in each repeat = 6 (10) sts in each repeat. Make sure that all the knit ribs in the pattern match the knit ribs in the cuff = 80 (88) sts total. Work around in k2, p2 ribbing for 4 in / 10 cm. Bind off in ribbing.

For the other cuff, pick up and knit 80 (88) sts along cast-on edge, picking up sts between the stitches since you'll be knitting in the opposite direction and so that the ribs will match. Divide sts onto dpn and work as for first cuff.

heidrun

My analytic mind breaks down the name Heidrun into its components: "heid" for bright, cloudless, and "run/runa" meaning secret wisdom. My prosaic husband and photographer would look up the mythological Heidrun and find out that it is the name of the goat that supplied mead in Valhalla. I'm sure he would have loved to date a Heidrun, until he met me, of course.

Sharing pattern elements with Fulla, the previous design, Heidrun is a completely different animal. Where Fulla is a more spectacular outfit, Heidrun is eye-catching in that sweet and utterly feminine way that some designs just are. Choose the one that matches your personality, or knit both for a choice depending on mood.

Sizes S (M, L)

Finished measurements

Chest	36¼ (38½, 41) in
	92 (98, 104) cm
Length	20½ (21¼, 22) in
	52 (54, 56) cm

Materials

Yarn Silky Wool (p. 14)

Yarn amounts 350 (400, 450) g

Needles US sizes 4 and 6 / 3.5 and 4 mm
16 in / 40 cm circular US size 4 / 3.5 mm
for neckband
Cable needle

Gauge 22 sts × 30 rows in stockinette on larger
needles = 4 × 4 in / 10 × 10 cm
Adjust needle sizes to obtain correct gauge if necessary.

Edge stitches The outermost st at each side is an edge st. Edge sts are included in the stitch counts and are always knitted unless otherwise specified.

Charts Looped Ring Chain Narrow, p. 66 and Looped Ring on Cross motif, p. 63.

Back
With smaller needles, cast on 92 sts (all sizes) and set up pattern.

Setup row, WS: Edge st, p1, * k2, p2, k8, p2, k2, p2, repeat from * 4 more times, ending the last repeat with an edge st instead of the last purl.
Row 2: Edge st, k1, * p2, k12, p2, k2, repeat from * 4 times. Repeat these 2 rows 3 times. There should now be 3 knit ribs on RS.

Change to larger needles and work: Edge st, k1, * 16 sts Looped Ring Chain Narrow chart, k2, repeat from * 4 times. The uncharted parts of the WS rows are worked knitting the knits and purling the purls.

Work 2 repeats and then continue knitting the knits and purling the purls. The center part of each repeat contains 8 sts of reverse stockinette. Work until piece measures 8¼ in / 21 cm.

Next, begin increasing: Edge st, k1, p2, k2, p8, k2, p2, k2, p2, k2 =10 sts ribbing, * RLI, p8, LLI, work 10 sts ribbing; repeat from * 2 more times, p8, k2, p2, k1, edge st = 6 sts increased across row. Repeat this increase row 1 (2, 3) more times every 14th (10th, 8th) row—there will be 2 more sts between the increases each time. The increased sts should be worked in reverse stockinette to form the center of the pattern panels. When all increases have been made, there will be 14 sts in each of the increased reverse stockinette sections and a total of 104 (110, 116) sts.

Continue without further shaping until piece measures 12¼ (12¾, 13) in / 31 (32, 33) cm.

Now begin working motifs following the chart for Looped Ring on Cross motif, at the center of the three reverse stockinette sections in the middle and, at the same time, begin shaping armholes: Bind off 3 sts at each side.

Now begin decreasing on WS: Edge st, p2, k2tog, work until 5 sts remain, ssk, p2, edge st. Decrease the same way on every other row 15 (14, 13) times total = 68 (76, 84) sts remain. Decreasing this way results in a 2-st stockinette rib framing the armhole. When armhole measures 8 (8¼, 8¾) in / 20 (21, 22) cm, place the center 30 sts on a holder and work each side separately. Shape shoulder with short rows, beginning at neck edge: Bind off 2 sts and work until 6 (7, 8) sts remain; turn and work back. Work 6 (7, 8) sts; turn and work back. Bind off remaining 17 (21, 25) sts for shoulder. Work other shoulder the same way, reversing shaping.

Front

Work as for back until armhole measures 6 (6½, 6¾) in / 15 (16, 17) cm. Place the center 20 sts on a holder and work each side separately. At neck edge, decrease 1 st inside the outermost 3 sts as for armhole on every other row 7 times. When armhole measures 8 (8¼, 8¾) in / 20 (21, 22) cm, shape shoulder with short rows, beginning at neck edge.

Work until 6 (7, 8) sts remain; turn and work back. Work 6 (7, 8) sts; turn and work back. Bind off remaining 17 (21, 25) sts for shoulder. Work other side the same way, reversing shaping.

Sleeves

With smaller needles, cast on 56 sts (all sizes) and set up pattern.

Setup row, WS: Edge st, p1, *k2, p2, k8, p2, k2, p2, repeat from * 2 times ending the last repeat with an edge st instead of the last purl.

Row 2: Edge st, k1, * p2, k12, p2, k2, repeat from * 2 times. Repeat these 2 rows 3 times. There should now be 3 knit ribs on RS.

Change to larger needles and work: Edge st, k1, *16 sts Looped Ring Chain Narrow chart, k2, repeat from * 2 times. The uncharted parts of the WS rows are worked knitting the knits and purling the purls.

Work 2 repeats and then continue knitting the knits and purling the purls—the center part of each repeat contains 8 sts of reverse stockinette. Work until sleeve is 8¼ in / 21 cm long.

Next, begin increasing: Edge st, k1, p2, k2, * RLI, p8, LLI, work 10 sts ribbing; repeat from * 1 more time, then end with RLI, p8, LLI, k2, p2, k1, edge st = 6 sts increased across row. Work this increase row 2 (3, 4) more times every 24th (18th, 14th) row—there will be 2 more sts between the increases each time. The increased sts should be worked in reverse stockinette to form the center of the pattern panels. When all increases have been made, there will be 74 (80, 86) sts on the needle.

When the sleeve is 16½ in / 42 cm long, shape sleeve cap by binding off 3 sts at each side. Now decrease 1 st inside 3 sts at each side, as for armhole, on every other row until 30 sts remain. Bind off.

Finishing

Block pieces. Undo bound-off sts and join shoulders with three-needle bind-off.

Mock Turtleneck: With smaller circular, pick up and knit 88 sts around the neck. Join and, making sure stockinette ribs are aligned at front and back, work around in k2, p2 ribbing for 3½ in / 9 cm. Bind off in ribbing.

Sew sleeve and side seams. Attach sleeves.

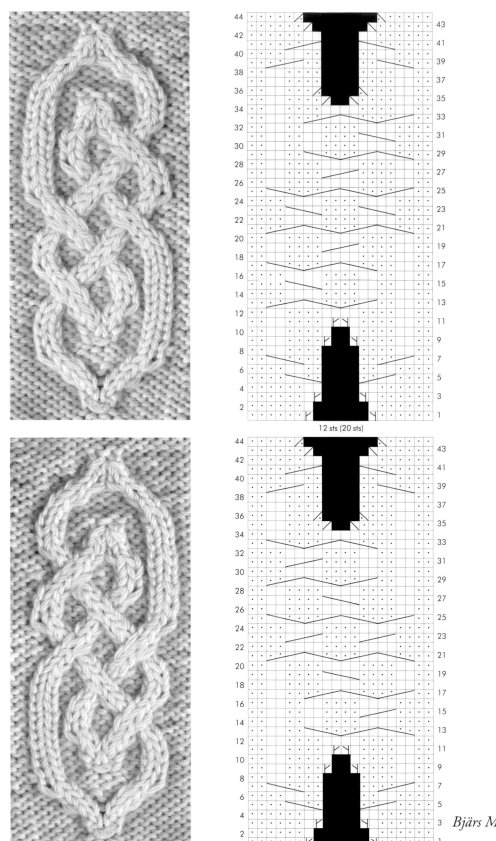

12 sts (20 sts)

12 sts (20 sts)

Bjärs Pointed Motif Left

Bjärs Motif Left & Right

74

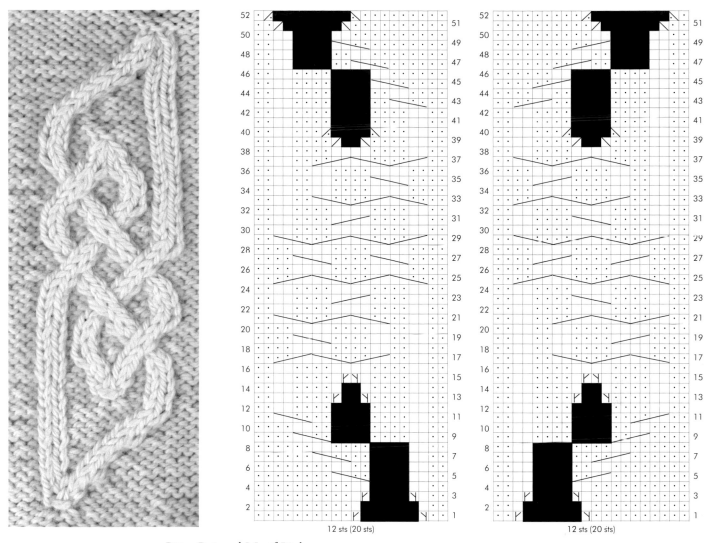

Bjärs Pointed Motif Right

The closely related pattern in the vignette that I have named the Bjärs panel is a looped ring chain where the small loops are joined in an asymmetrical manner. It was analyzed in *Viking Patterns for Knitting*. For this book, I made a motif version of the same basic pattern, with the cut-off bands joined to form a twisted figure eight. As you can see, the person who made this decoration on a page from the Book of Kells had the same design idea, so I took it a bit further and included both a rounded and a pointed variety.

ODDRUN

This sweater comes in two versions: The extrovert version has slits and paired motifs at the hips and at the neckline. A more introvert, but just as pretty, version is toned down to just the motifs. Feel free to express your own personal degree of -trovertness. You could even go all out and add slits on the sleeves as well. Whatever you choose, you're bound to look gorgeous.

The first part of the name is the Icelandic oddr, *"point, spear-point, arrow-point." As second element in a name,* -rún *should be understood as having the meaning, "she who possesses hidden knowledge". Hidden or not, I've always felt that knowledge is a great weapon.*

Sizes   S (M, L, XL)

Finished measurements
Chest   34¾ (38½, 42½, 46½) in
             88 (98, 108, 118) cm
Length   21¾ (22, 22½, 22¾) in
             55 (56, 57, 58) cm

Materials
Yarn   Silky Wool (p. 14)
Yarn amounts 300 (350, 400, 450) g
Needles US sizes 4 and 6 / 3.5 and 4 mm
             Short circular US size 4 / 3.5 mm for
             neck edging
             Cable needle
Optional: Crochet hook US size E-4 / 3.5 mm
             for edgings

Gauge   22 sts × 30 sts in stockinette on larger
             needles = 4 × 4 in / 10 × 10 cm
Adjust needle sizes to obtain correct gauge if necessary.

Edge Stitches The outermost st at each side is an edge st. Edge sts are included in the stitch counts and are always knitted unless otherwise specified. When charted pattern is placed near a slit, the stitch nearest the slit is worked as an edge st even if it is not marked as such on the chart.

Note Increase and decrease inside edge st on WS (p. 184).

Charts Bjärs Pointed Motif Left and Right pp. 74–75. The motifs are placed so that they open downwards at the lower edge and on the sleeves, and upwards at the neck.

Back

Without slits: With smaller needles, cast on 96 (106, 116, 126) sts and knit 7 rows. Change to larger needles and work in reverse stockinette. After 4 rows, set up motif: Place a marker 33 (37, 40, 44) sts in from each side (these markers should be moved up as you knit). Work the Bjärs motif left over the last 11 sts before the marker but omit the last st on the chart. Work the Bjärs motif right over the first 11 sts after the marker, omitting the first st of the chart so that there will be 2 reverse stockinette sts between the stockinette ribs higher up on the chart. On Row 20, begin decreasing 1 st at each side and decrease again on Rows 28, 36, 44, and 52 = 86 (96, 106, 116) sts remain.

With slits, left side: With smaller needles, cast on 34 (38, 41, 45) sts and knit 7 rows. Change to larger needles and reverse stockinette. After 4 rows, work Bjärs motif left over the last 12 sts of the row. On Row 20, begin deceasing 1 st at the side without the cable pattern. After completing Row 27, set piece aside.

With slits, right side: Work as for left side but place the Bjärs motif right over the first 12 sts of the row.

With slits, center: With smaller needles, cast on 32 (34, 38, 40) sts and knit 7 rows. Change to larger needles and reverse stockinette. After 4 rows, work the Bjärs motif right over the first 12 sts of the row and Bjärs motif left over the last 12 sts. *On Row 28 join the pieces, eliminating the edge sts at the slits as the same time as decreasing at the sides:* Work the right side and begin with edge st, k2tog and end piece with ssk; begin center section with k2tog and end with ssk. Begin left side with k2tog and end with ssk, edge st. There should be 2 purl sts between the outermost stockinette sts of the two motifs straight above.

Decrease at each side only, with k1, k2tog at beginning

of row and ssk, k1 at end on Rows 36, 44, and 52. There should now be 86 (96, 106, 116) sts remaining. Continue in reverse stockinette. Place a marker directly above each slit and move marker up on each row.

Both versions: When the piece measures 8 in / 20 cm, begin increasing as follows: Edge st, RLI, work to first marker, RLI after marker, work to second marker, LLI before marker, work to edge st, LLI, edge st. Increase the same way on every 8th row 3 (4, 4, 5) times total = 98 (112, 122, 136) sts. Now increase only between the markers another 4 times = 106 (120, 130, 144) sts.

At the same time, when piece measures 14¼ (14¼, 15, 15) in / 36 (36, 38, 38) cm, shape armholes by first binding off 3 (4, 5, 6) sts at each side and then 2 sts at each side 1 (2, 3, 4) times. Now decrease 1 st at each side on every other row 8 (10, 10, 12) times = 80 (84, 88, 92) sts remain.

When armhole measures 7½ (8, 8¼, 8¾) in / 19 (20, 21, 22) cm, bind off the center 32 (32, 34, 34) sts and work each side separately. Shape shoulder beginning at neck edge: Bind off another 2 sts at neck edge and work until 8 (8, 9, 9) sts remain; turn and work back. Work 8 (8, 9, 9) sts; turn and work back. Bind off remaining 22 (24, 25, 27) sts for shoulder. Work the other side the same way, reversing shaping.

Front

Work as for back until ¾ in / 2 cm before armhole. Place a marker at the center and begin working motifs placed as follows: over 11 sts before the marker, work following chart for Bjärs right, omitting the last st; over 11 sts after the marker, work Bjärs left, omitting the first st on chart so that there will be 2 purl sts between the outermost stockinette ribs of the two motifs. *At the same time,* shape the armhole as for the back: bind off 3 (4, 5, 6) sts at each side and then 2 sts at each side 1 (2, 3, 4) times. Now decrease 1 st at each side on every other row 8 (10, 10, 12) times = 80 (84, 88, 92) sts remain.

Without slits: After completing charted rows, work 2 (4, 4, 6) rows reverse stockinette. On the next row, place the center 22 (22, 24, 24) sts on a holder for neck. Work each side separately. At neck edge, decrease 1 st on every other row 7 times. When armhole measures 7½ (8, 8¼, 8¾) in / 19 (20, 21, 22) cm, shape shoulder beginning at neck edge: work until 8 (8, 9, 9) sts remain; turn and work back. Work 8 (8, 9, 9) sts; turn and work back. Bind off remaining 22 (24, 25, 27) sts for shoulder. Work the other side the same way, reversing shaping.

With slits: After completing Row 26, divide the piece at the center and work each side separately.

Left side: Cast on a new edge st at the center front and continue as set. After completing charted rows, work 2 (4, 4, 6) rows in reverse stockinette. On the next row, place 13 (13, 14, 14) sts at front edge on a holder. At neck edge, decrease 1 st on every other row 6 times. When armhole measures 7½ (8, 8¼, 8¾) in / 19 (20, 21, 22) cm, shape shoulder beginning at neck edge: work until 8 (8, 9, 9) sts remain; turn and work back. Work 8 (8, 9, 9) sts; turn and work back. Bind off remaining 22 (24, 25, 27) sts for shoulder.

Right side: Work as for left side, reversing shaping.

Sleeves

With smaller needles, cast on 50 (52, 54, 56) sts and knit 7 rows. Change to larger needles and work 4 rows in reverse stockinette. Place a marker at center of row. Now work Bjärs motif left over the last 11 sts before the center, omitting the last st on the chart. Work Bjärs motif right over the first 11 sts after the center, omitting the first st on the chart so that there will be 2 sts reverse stockinette sts between the outermost stockinette ribs of the two motifs. After completing charted rows, continue in reverse stockinette and begin increasing 1 st at each side on every 6th row 13 (14, 15, 16) times = 76 (80, 84, 88) sts.

When sleeve is 16½ in / 42 cm long, shape sleeve cap by first binding off 3 (4, 5, 6) sts at each side. Next, decrease 1 st at each side until 32 sts remain. Bind off 2 sts at the beginning of the next 8 rows. Bind off remaining 16 sts.

Finishing

Block pieces. Undo bound-off sts and join shoulders with three-needle bind-off.

Neck Edging: With circular, beginning at the slit, pick up and knit 101 (105, 109, 113) sts around neck. Knit 1 round and then bind off.

Slit Edgings: With smaller needles, pick up and knit 23–26 sts along each side of a slit. The exact number of sts isn't important but there should be the same number of sts picked up along each slit. Mark the center of the slit. Knit until 2 sts before marker, ssk, k2tog, knit to end of row. Bind off. If you prefer, you can work a row of single crochet along each of the slit edges.

Attach sleeves. Sew sleeve and side seams.

Little Knot & Fourknot

Neither the Little Knot, nor the Fourknot are knots in the strict sense of the word. The Little Knot consists of two braided rings, while the Fourknot is a ring with four twists, keeping the over-under systematic sequence. Both can be oriented two ways, the Little Knot with one or two rings meeting the baseline, and the Fourknot either balancing on one of the loops or resting on one of the sides. Both these knots share the property of being suited for knitting in only one of their manifestations, but on the other hand, the variations are almost limitless.

Both knots are related to the swastika, and they can all be interpreted as symbols of the sun. In the Western world, the Nazis tarnished the reputation of the swastika, but this is not so in the Orient, where the symbol is frequently used. Looking at various ornamental traditions, the direction of the arms seems to be arbitrary, and attempts have been made to "resurrect" the mirrored version of the Nazi swastika by assigning a different name to it: Fylfot. Generally, however, this term is used for more rounded versions of the symbol, but regardless of angularity, they belong to the same "family".

"Whirling Log" is the term used for mirrored swastikas in Navajo Indian woven blanket patterns. Some weavers turn it into a Little Knot, and the close relationship between the swastika, the Little Knot and the Fourknot is obvious in the abundance of versions I have found (see page 96).

Little Knot

The Little Knot is perhaps better known as a Solomon's knot, probably because it used to be a recurrent ornament in synagogues. But it can be found all over the world, and according to some sources it's even traceable back to Stone Age carvings. It appears in the Mediterranean in both Roman and Byzantine mosaics and on stone friezes. In Islamic culture, it can be seen decorating the walls and ceilings of both mosques and palaces, but I have found many other Little Knot manifestations: on a 15th century Spanish or possibly North African silk fabric, on a circa 1340 painting of the death bed of Alexander the Great, and as corner motif on a wood engraving from the same period, to name a few. Mongols, Africans, Aztecs and North American Indians all provide examples of various Little Knot designs.

Yet another name is "Comacine knot", since it is believed to have been used as a symbol for the Comacines,

Viking age metal plaque with Little Knot ornaments from Sorunda, Sweden

Italian stonemasons in early medieval Lombardy before the Langobardic invasion, and later also used in Langobardic ornamentation. The Comacines, allegedly the founders of the Freemason organization, attributed a mystic meaning to the knot as a symbol of eternal movement and the intertwining of time and space.

You may also have come across the name "Love Knot", a rather obvious symbolic interpretation of two intertwined rings, but this is a name that has been given to several other knots as well, so to avoid ambiguity I don't use it in this book.

The basic Little Knot in its rounded version was covered in my *Viking Patterns for Knitting* book. For the pointed variety, see the Four Band Braid, p. 154.

The Little Knot was a cherished element in Viking age ornamentation, so artifacts like the ones shown here and on the previous page are not hard to find. But as you can guess from the drawing of an Anglo-Saxon mount, it was likely held in high esteem by the peoples of the British Isles as well.

It is also frequently found in Roman mosaics from the first century AD. Shown below is a beautiful example with a tri-colored band coupled to a heart-shaped ornament.

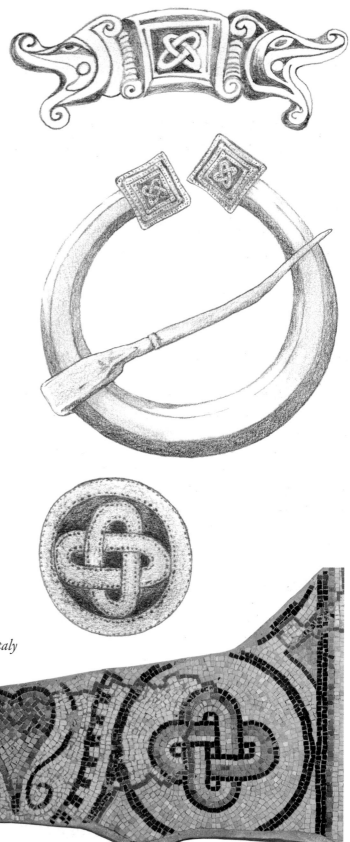

Left: Decor on rein guide, Björkö, Sweden
Top right: Anglo-Saxon mount,
Bidford-on-Avon, England
Next down: Pennanular brooch, Visby,
Gotland, Sweden
Right: Bronze pendant, Uppåkra, Sweden
Below right: Roman mosaic on display in
Museo Nazionale Paleocristiano, Aquileia, Italy

The Langobards made use of it in many ways; the photo shows it in several versions on a buckle now on display in Cividale del Friuli, Italy.

Langobardic buckle, Museo Archeologico Nazionale di Cividale del Friuli, Italy

The Youruba people utilize the Little Knot on all sorts of objects. They refer to it as Ibo, and it's associated with royalty. An ivory ornament in the shape of a ram's head, worn attached to a ceremonial garment from the 17th or possibly 18th century, is just one of many examples I have found (see page 86). Other African sources include the Nigerian Hausa culture, where it's known as the Kano knot, named after the Kingdom of Kano which existed from around the turn of the last millennium and into the 19th century. The

Kano knot adorns façades, as single elements or as part of an all-over decoration. Islam introduced the use of large, full-length shirts with traditional embroideries, and those frequently included the Kano knot.

The Ashanti people of Ghana traditionally used distinctive pieces of cloth as burial shrouds. This is the origin of the Adinkra tradition, a set of symbols imprinted on e.g. fabric. In this symbolic system the little knot means "one bad makes all look bad". Further south, in the Kuba culture, the men weave fabrics that are then embroidered by the women, using raphia bast fiber to produce a velvety surface. They have come to be known as Kasai velvets, today sought-after collectables.

Above: Detail of embroidery on a 19th century shirt, Hausa tribe, Nigeria
Right: Kano house, Nigeria

To the Kubas themselves, these fabrics have no practical use, but a quite significant ceremonial function; various kinds of intertwined motifs come together in rhythmic constellations. The words "embroidered jazz" comes to mind, at least to my mind. Here's an example with an elongated little knot from a Kasai velvet.

Detail of Kasai velvet, Kuba, Congo

Continue eastward to Somalia, and you will discover the Little Knot on a number of traditional headrests. Cross the Atlantic and you will find the Aztecs using it as a symbol of motion. A stone relief excavated in Tajín, Mexico, depicting a human sacrifice scene, includes the Little Knot. The depicted stone fragment from Nicaragua is probably Mayan in origin.

As if the above is not enough to indicate the global appeal of the Little Knot, check out this pendant from the Khalkha Mongols, where the main Little Knot motif is accompanied by a pair of Eternal Knots (p. 162).

The rings can be stretched out to the point where they become straight lines rather than rings, as in this shield ornament on one of the Lewis Chessmen; Medieval Scottish chess pieces, carved in whale bone. Another example from just after the Viking age can be found on a belt buckle from Haute-Savoie, France (shown on next page).

Above: Detail of a pre-Hispanic carving at El Tajín, Mexico
Below left: Mayan stone fragment, Nicaragua
Below middle: Chess piece, Lewis, Scotland,
Great Britain
Below right: Pendant, Kahlka tribe, Mongolia

Little Knot Extended

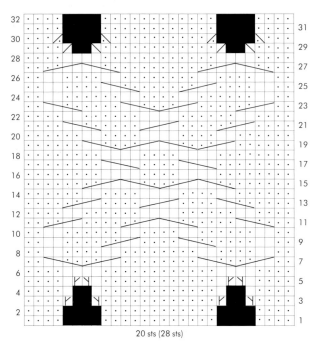

20 sts (28 sts)

Merovingian belt buckle, Haute-Savoie, France

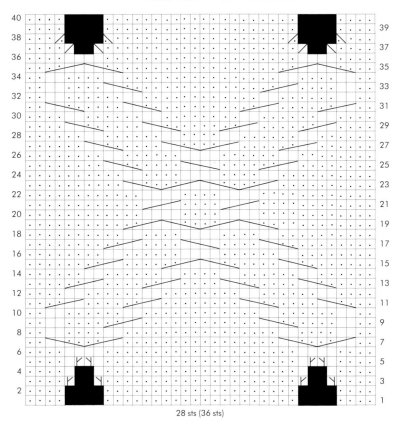

Little Knot More Extended

28 sts (36 sts)

When knitted, the Little Knot can be varied in many ways without affecting the basic shape. You can change the size, and the endings can be made either centered or directional. The one below has centered endings, the one to the right directional endings.

Little Knot More Stretched

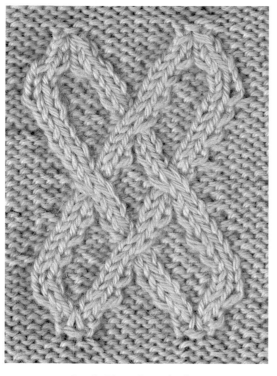

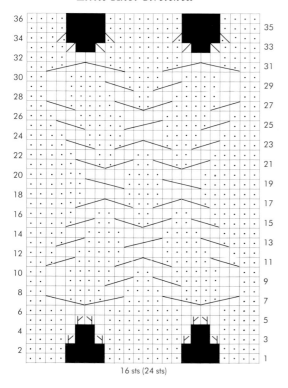

Little Knot Stretched

Comb
Saramaccan tribe,
Suriname

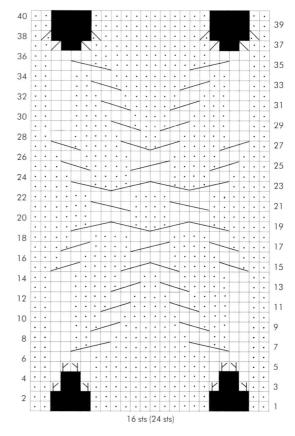

16 sts (24 sts)

16 sts (24 sts)

LOFN

Lofn is a Norse Goddess of Love. Her task is to make way for unions between men and women, and her name is possibly the origin of the English word "love". The motif I used consists of two inseparably interlocked rings and is thus sometimes referred to as a Love Knot, but as discussed earlier in this chapter, it is just one of several knots that have been called Love Knot.

Regardless of how you name the knot, knitting this scarf could be a deed of love, for yourself, a lover or a beloved child. The Little Knot is a symbol of good fortune and who wouldn't want that, in life as well as in your knitting.

Finished measurements
8 in / 20 cm wide and 71 in / 180 cm long

Materials
Yarn	SensuAl (p. 14)
Yarn amounts	250 g, 1 ball is enough for just less than 2 pattern blocks
Needles	US size 10 / 6 mm
	32 in / 80 cm circular US size 10 / 6 mm
	Cable needle
Optional	Crochet hook US size J-10 / 6 mm for crocheted edging

Gauge 12 sts × 18 rows in stockinette
= 4 × 4 in / 10 × 10 cm
Adjust needle size to obtain correct gauge if necessary.

Edge Stitches The outermost st at each side is an edge st. Edge sts are included in the stitch counts and are always knitted unless otherwise specified.

Chart Little Knot Extended, p. 84.

Cast on 28 sts and knit 3 rows; the 1st row = WS. Now work in reverse stockinette, beginning on RS: * Purl 1 row, knit 1 row. On the next row, begin the motif centered on the piece. Continue to work the 4 sts at each side in reverse stockinette. After completing the 32 charted rows, work another 3 rows in reverse stockinette (the last row is purled on RS). The first block is now complete. Repeat from *. The

pattern is designed so that the next block's RS is above the WS of the previous block. Continue as set until there are 8 complete blocks and the scarf is almost 71 in / 180 cm long. Finish with 3 knit rows and then bind off.

Edging along long side: Pick up sts along one long side by inserting the circular needle tip into each knot created by the edge sts. Simply pick up each knot and put onto needle. Picking up sts this way produces a reversible result. Knit 2 rows and then bind off, making sure that the bind-off is loose but neat. Work the edging for the other side the same way.

If you prefer, you can edge the scarf with 1 row of single crochet along each long edge.

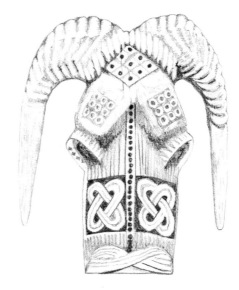

Carved ram's head, 17th–19th century, Yoruba tribe, Benin

By inserting a ring through the "arms" of the Little Knot, you create another variation. The examples shown on the next page are a 19th century carved Yoruba calabash box, and on yet another Lewis chess piece. This creates a motif which is basically the same as the Large Knot (see p. 159). Here's a knitted variety with elongated arms, followed by a version attached to a cable.

Little Knot & Ring

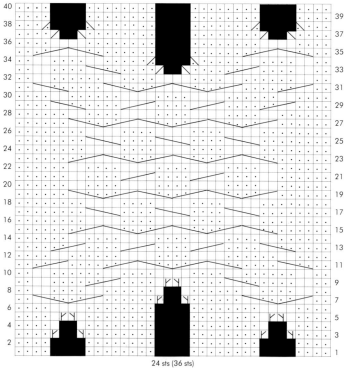

24 sts (36 sts)

Little Knot & Ring on Cable

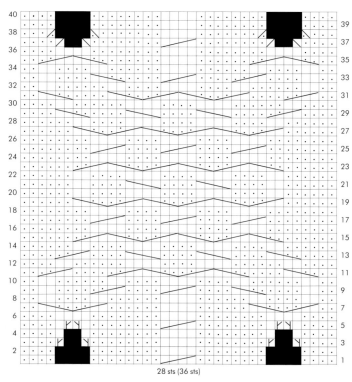

28 sts (36 sts)

In a 16th century embroidery pattern book by German author Peter Quentel, I found a page with a border of Little Knots with bands intertwined. On a side note, the same page also showed a border of Linked Rings. I discovered a Little Knot and Ring motif used as a beadwork decoration on a ceremonial garment from the Yoruba tribe. This type of motif can also be found in the art of the Nigerian Hausa tribe.

Fourknot

The Fourknot is also known as a Shield Knot. Just like the Little Knot, it is a common symbol in virtually every civilization in the world, tracing its origin back several millennia. The cardinal points were important in most ancient cultures, and the Fourknot has often been used to represent them, hence the sometimes used English name "Earth Square". One of the oldest discoveries is from Mesopotamia and believed to be some four thousand years old.

In classical antiquity it can be found in both mosaics and on stone reliefs all over the eastern Mediterranean; later

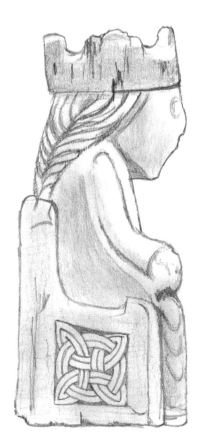

Above left: Calabash box, Yoruba, Nigeria
Above: Carved chair, Nigeria
Below left: Chess piece, Lewis, Scotland, Great Britain
Below: Roman mosaic, The Basilica of Aquileia, Italy

also spreading further west. The Langobards seem to have been particularly fond of it. It is also a recurring ornament among African peoples in Benin, Nigeria, Congo and Ethiopia. Carved into a Nigerian chair, the Fourknot is surrounded by Large Knots (previous page).

Stone with carved Fourknot, France

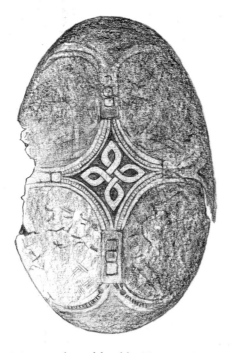

Tortoise shaped buckle, Troms, Norway

Cox mound style gorget, Missouri, USA

Having spent a couple of my younger years in Missouri, I was especially pleased to find Fourknots as the predominant adornment of gorgets, commonly found in grave mounds of southeastern Indian tribes from the Mississippi period, AD 900–1500.

These are large Atlantic seashells worn around the neck and typically carved in a very distinctive way: In the middle a circle, or a sun symbol, with a cross inside, surrounded by a Fourknot, generally carved with two pairs of parallel lines joining the loops. Above the lines woodpecker heads with their beaks oriented counter-clockwise. This is interpreted as a representation of the world. The central section shows the sun, shining over the camp fire in the village center.

Some scholars suggest that it is the Fourknot that symbolizes the world we live in, with the woodpeckers indicating cardinal points, while others claim it to be a representation of the litter used to carry the chiefs around. Support for the former theory comes from present day Chickasaw dancers, who spontaneously assert it to show the path of dancers around the town square in the beginning of ceremonies.

In both Nordic and Insular cultures, the Shield Knot is very common. As the name suggests, it was thought to have protective powers. Some scholars claim it to represent Jörmungandr, the Midgard serpent that holds the world together in Norse mythology. Christianity has named it the St. John's Cross. The drawings show some examples of Viking Fourknot decorations.

Fourknots with a ring woven into the loops are common, and seemingly especially favored by the Langobards, but the African Yoruba and Hausa people also frequently contribute to my "collection". The Vikings, or possibly their successors (dating is a bit uncertain), used this variation on a picture stone presently kept inside the Rute Church, Gotland, Sweden, close to where it was originally found. Some sources claim that the Vikings believed this symbol protected them against sorcery.

Picture stone, Rute church, Gotland, Sweden

The basic Fourknot design was covered in my *Viking Patterns for Knitting* book, but a less common variation combines a Fourknot with a Little Knot. I have found an incomplete example on an Egyptian embroidery, dated between the late 12th and mid-13th century and in a typical Islamic style. Made this way, the motif is very similar to the Hausa Knot (see p. 160).

Islamic embroidery 12th century, Egypt

In the depicted arch decoration which stems from the summit of Kidane Meheret of Mount Zion, Ethiopia, there is a further development: The ring has become a Fourknot, creating a Fourknot intertwined with a Fourknot.

Vaulted ceiling, Mount Zion, Ethiopia

Little Knot & Fourknot

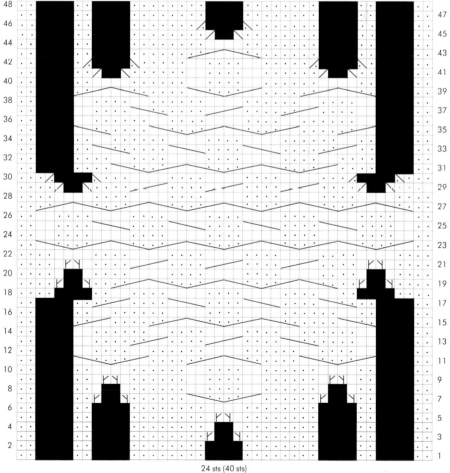

24 sts (40 sts)

JORD

If, like me, you like your sweaters to make a statement (why else would you buy a book like this one?) combining garment and jewelry can sometimes be a problem; a pleasant one, perhaps, but still. Jord can solve this problem most elegantly: With the cut-off Fourknots guarding the neckline and the cuffs, this sweater is automatically bejeweled, and the exquisite LinSilk yarn adds to the appeal.

Jord is the Earth Goddess, mother of Thor, the God of Thunder, and I'm pretty sure our model is pleased with the name I chose for "her" sweater.

Sizes S (M, L, XL)

Finished measurements

Chest	34 (37½, 41, 44½) in
	86 (95, 104, 113) cm
Length	21 (21¾, 22½, 23¼) in
	53 (55, 57, 59) cm

Materials
Yarn LinSilk (p. 14)
Yarn amounts 350 (400, 450, 500) g
Needles US sizes 6 and 7 / 4 and 4.5 mm
Cable needle

Gauge 18 sts × 26 rows in reverse stockinette on larger needles = 4 × 4 in / 10 × 10 cm
Adjust needle sizes to obtain correct gauge if necessary.

Edge Stitches The outermost st at each side is an edge st. Edge sts are included in the stitch counts and are always knitted unless otherwise specified.

Note Do not splice yarn at the neck edge and at slit edges. Increase and decrease on WS, p. 184.

Charts Fourknot Cutoff Up, p. 95 and Fourknot Cutoff Down, p. 94.

Back
With smaller needles, cast on 78 (86, 94, 102) sts and knit 7 rows in garter st; the 1st row = WS. Change to larger nee- dles and work in reverse stockinette. When piece measures 1½ (2, 2½, 2¾) in / 4 (5, 6, 7) cm, decrease 1 st at each side (inside edge st) on every 6th row 6 times = 66 (74, 82, 90) sts. Continue as set, and, when piece measures 7 (7½, 8, 8¼) in / 18 (19, 20, 21) cm, increase 1 st at each side on every 4th row 8 times = 82 (90, 98, 106) sts.

Armhole Shaping: When piece measures 13½ (13¾, 14¼, 14½) in / 34 (35, 36, 37) cm, shape armhole by first bind- ing off 4 sts at each side (all sizes) and then 2 sts at each side 1 (1, 2, 2) times. Next, inside edge st, decrease 1 st at each side on every other row 3 (5, 5, 7) times = 64 (68, 72, 76) sts remain. When armhole measures 7½ (8, 8¼, 8¾) in / 19 (20, 21, 22) cm, bind off the center 24 (24, 26, 26) sts and work each side separately.

Shoulder Shaping: Shape shoulder with short rows, be- ginning at neck edge: bind off 2 sts at neck edge and then work until 6 (7, 7, 8) sts remain; turn and work back. Work 6 (7, 8, 8) sts; turn and work back. Bind off remaining 18 (20, 21, 23) sts for shoulder. Work the other side the same way, reversing shaping.

Front
Work as for back until you are ready to work the last in- crease at the sides. *At the same time* as working this increase, begin charted motif Fourknot Cutoff up, centered at front. *Note* that 4 sts are increased within the motif.
Also at the same time, shape armhole by first binding off 4 sts at each side and then 2 sts at each side 1 (1, 2, 2) times. Next, inside edge st, decrease 1 st at each side on ev- ery other row 3 (5, 5, 7) times = 68 (72) 76 (80) sts remain. On Row 19 of the pattern, divide front at the center as

follows: Work to the cable crossing, cross the 4 center sts *but work only the first 2 of these sts*. Place the last 2 sts of the cable and the rest of the sts on a holder. It is important to "break" at the center of the cable for a neat edge at the start of the V-neck.

Left half: Complete the motif. From Row 21, work the st nearest the divided cable as an edge st and the 2 sts inside this edge st in stockinette. Shape neck by decreasing on the WS, inside 3 sts at edge, on every other row 13 (13, 14, 14) times. When armhole measures 7½ (8, 8¼, 8¾) in/ 19 (20, 21, 22) cm, shape shoulder, beginning at neck edge: work until 6 (7, 8, 8) sts remain; turn and work back. Work 3 sts at front edge + 6 (7, 8, 8) sts; turn and work back. Using a separate strand of yarn, bind off 18 (20, 21, 23) sts for shoulder; 3 sts remain at neck edge.

Neckband: Cast on a new edge st at shoulder and continue working over these 4 sts in stockinette until the strip easily stretches to center back neck.

Right half: Work as for left half, reversing shaping.

Sleeves

Left half: With smaller needles, cast on 21 (22, 23, 24) sts and knit 7 rows in garter st, except on one side (at the slit) where you work 2 stockinette sts inside the edge st. The 1st row = WS; don't forget to purl the 2 stockinette sts on WS. After completing the 7 rows, change to larger needles and work in reverse stockinette over the garter stitch section; the stockinette rib continues as set. Work as set for 2½ in / 6 cm and set piece aside.

Right half: Work as for left half, reversing rib placement.

Joining the pieces: Join the two pieces with the stockinette ribs facing each other. Knit the motif following the chart, Fourknot Cutoff down, beginning on Row 3 of the chart. Note that 4 sts are decreased within the motif. After completing motif, the sleeve should measure 5¼ in / 13 cm and 38 (40, 42, 44) sts remain. Now begin shaping sleeve by increasing 1 st inside edge st at each side on every 6th row 11 (12, 13, 14) times = 60 (64, 68, 72) sts.

Sleeve Cap: When sleeve is 15¾ in / 40 cm long, shape sleeve cap by first binding off 4 (4, 5, 5) sts at each side and then 2 sts at each side. Next, decrease 1 st inside edge st at each side on every other row until 30 sts remain. Bind off 2 sts each at the beginning of the next 8 rows and then bind off remaining 14 sts.

Finishing

Block pieces. Undo bound-off sts and join shoulders with three-needle bind-off. Join short ends of neckband at center back and sew band down along back neck as invisibly as possible. Attach sleeves. Sew sleeve and side seams.

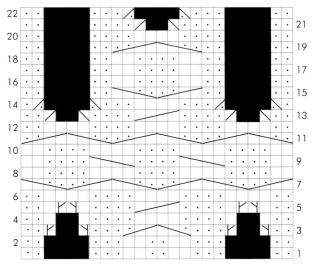

Fourknot Cutoff Down

16 sts (increased to 24 and decreased to 12)

Ceiling decor from the Abbey of Santa María la Real de Las Huelgas, Spain

Opening one of the loops allows for the Fourknot to be attached to bands or cables. And just as with separate loops, the openings can face upwards or downwards, left or right. Horizontal attached versions can be found in my *Viking Patterns for Knitting* book, so I decided to complete the picture by including "vertical growth" in this one:

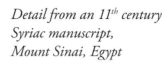

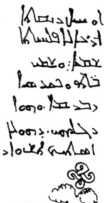

Detail from an 11th century Syriac manuscript, Mount Sinai, Egypt

Fourknot Cutoff Up

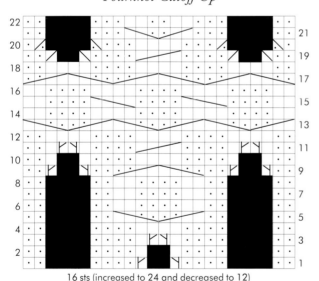

16 sts (increased to 24 and decreased to 12)

Capital from The Chapel of Our Lady, Menton, France

16th century Ethiopian processional cross

The kinship between the Little Knot and the Fourknot and their relationship to the swastika is clearly visible in the diverse collection below, and searching for ornamental expressions from around the globe has been a rewarding experience indeed. These examples represent just a small fraction of all my discoveries.

Animal ornamentation on a box brooch from Gotland, Sweden. The twined bodies emit a strong sense of movement. It is easy to imagine taking this design a step further and making it a Little Knot or a Fourknot. I have found very similar motifs in e.g. Irish manuscripts and as a border ornament on the above 14th to 15th century Ethiopian Bible.

Making a Fourknot directional gives it a swastika-like appearance. This example is a Rangoli, a contemporary form of northern India street art: You create patterns with sand, flour or chalk, generally on the street outside your house, to honor your guests and greet them welcome. In southern India, this tradition is called Kolam.

The spear knob ornament, also from Gotland, doesn't convey quite as much movement, but the Fourknot is obvious.

Punched into the bottom of a bowl, a part of the Saint Ninian's Treasure found on Shetland, an intricate type of fylfot clearly points towards the swastika (above left).

A spiraled fylfot decorating the Conchan Cross on Isle of Man shows another transition path from swastika to Fourknot (above right).

The Anglo Saxon shoulder clasps from Taplow, England have an open version of the Fourknot, i.e. the loops are not closed.

Here's another Rangoli, this time a Little Knot combined with a swastika.

On the Langobardic buckle, on display in the Museo Archeologico Nazionale in Cividale del Friuli, Italy, two of the Fourknot loops are left open.

The Aztec movement sign from Tabasco, Mexico, shows how closing the arms of the swastika will produce a Little Knot.

Threeknot

Threeknot, trefoil, triquetra... The many names for this symbol can serve as an indication of its popularity. At the emerging stages of my Viking Knits Project, I thought it impossible to recreate in knitting, but luckily I was later able to prove myself wrong—this is simply a too widespread and powerful design not to be used in knitwear.

The Threeknot is commonly interpreted as representing the trinity of body, mind and soul. Christianity specifically attributes it to the Holy Trinity, but long before Christian times it was considered to have a strong symbolic significance. In Celtic mythology, it is believed to symbolize the Goddess, she who reigns over the Earth, the Sea and the Heavens.

In Norse mythology, the number three is used to represent the god Odin, typically in the form of a Valknut (three interlocked triangles), a triskele (three interlocked spirals) or a triquetra, as in the above chapter vignette. On the depicted 11th century coin from the reign of the Danish king Knut (Canute), it's hard to establish if the ornament is actually a triskele or a triquetra (below).

The motif is common in all corners of the Viking world, including its eastern boundaries, a fact that became available to Westerners as information about Viking age Eastern Europe and Russia finally started to reach us "outsiders" in the last couple of decades. This Threeknot adorned pendant from Gnezdovo, Russia, is one example. "Closer to home" the Threeknot appears on the woman figure from Tissø, Denmark, and on the small fragment from Sandmúle, Iceland.

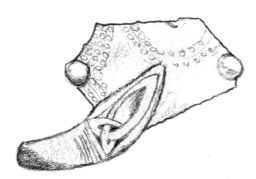

Left: Coin from king Canute or Hardeknut, found in Denmark
Above: Fragment from Sandmúle, Iceland
Above right: Pendant from Gnezdovo, Russia
Right: Woman figure from Tissø, Denmark

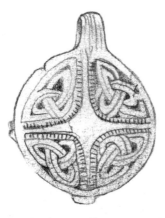

Pendant from Öland, Sweden

The ornamentation on a cross from Yorkshire, England ends with three Threeknots (not shown); perhaps the craftsman believed that three times three multiplies the power of the symbol? On the small pendant from Öland, Sweden, the craftsman has included four Threeknots, which, by the same logic, should be extremely potent. Both three and four are numbers considered to be very powerful in Christian as well as Pre-Christian times. And just as is the case with the Little Knot, the Threeknot frequently acts as the center point of the designs.

This is not the case with the rune stone in the below photo, but there are so many intriguing things going on in the ornamentation that I just had to include the photo in the book. And with four Threeknots visible, this was the chapter to show it in.

I haven't had many chances to display objects from the Sami culture in connection with the Viking Knits project, so I was thrilled to discover this Sami drum hammer with a Threeknot as its major design element.

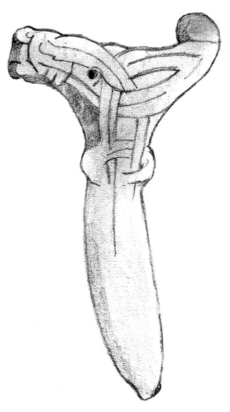

Left: Rune stone placed outside the Frösunda church, Vallentuna, Sweden
Above: Sami shaman's hammer, Sweden

Threeknot Upwards

Threeknot Downwards

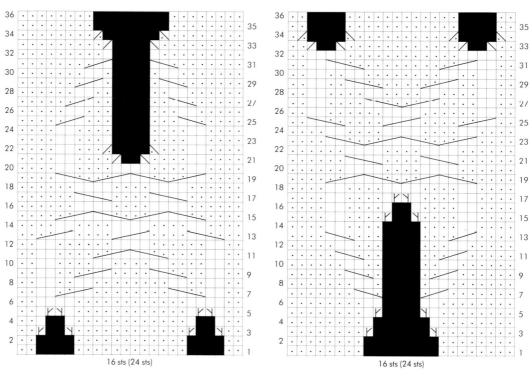

16 sts (24 sts)

16 sts (24 sts)

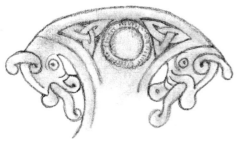

Above: Viking age metal mount from Gotland, Sweden
Left: Detail on an 8ᵗʰ century Anglo-Saxon disc brooch, England

EIR

Eir is the goddess of healing. The triquetra is a symbol often used for the trinity of body, mind and spirit, so combining the two is very appropriate for healing purposes, which is exactly the effect knitting often has on me.

I've made two versions of Eir in very different yarns: one my "firstborn" all-time favorite Silky Wool and the other in ViSilk, a more recent and festive addition to my yarn line with both shine and drape. The choice of yarn provides a distinct "personality" for each version, but I think both are lovely. And this knitted version of the triquetra is particularly attractive, placed decorating the gussets and the sleeves where it's highly visible.

Sizes S (M, L, XL)

Finished measurements
Chest   34 (37, 39¾, 41½) in
         86 (94, 101, 108) cm
Length   21 (21¾, 22½, 23¼) in
         53 (55, 57, 59) cm

Yarn ViSilk *or* Silky Wool (p. 14)
Yarn amounts 200 (250, 250, 300) g

Needles US size 6 / 4 mm (circular recommended)
Cable needle

Gauge 21 sts × 28 rows in stockinette
= 4 × 4 in / 10 × 10 cm
Adjust needle size to obtain correct gauge if necessary.

Edge Stitches The outermost st at each side is an edge st. Edge sts are included in the stitch counts and are always knitted unless otherwise specified.

Chart Three Knot Up, p. 99.

Front
Cast on 124 (132, 140, 148) sts and knit 7 rows in garter st. *Set up pattern as follows:* Edge st, k1, work 24 sts for gusset following the chart, work 72 (80, 88, 96) sts stockinette, 24 gusset sts following chart, k1, edge st. Shape gusset on WS rows as shown on chart. After charted rows are complete, 80 (88, 96, 104) sts remain; the piece should now be 6¼ in /16 cm long. Work 6 rows as set.

Place a marker at each side of the center 30 sts and increase as follows: Edge st, k2, LLI, work until 1 st before the first marker, RLI, k2, LLI, work until 1 st before the second marker, RLI, k2, LLI, work until 3 sts remain and end with RLI, edge st. Repeat this increase row on every 6th row another 4 times = 100 (108, 116, 124) sts. When piece measures 13¾ (14¼, 14½, 15) in / 35 (36, 37, 38) cm, shape armhole by binding off 8 sts at each side = 84 (92, 100, 108) sts remain. Set piece aside.

Sleeve Bands*:* Cast on 73 (77, 81, 85) sts and knit 7 rows in garter st. On the next row, bind off 8 sts at the front edge of the sleeve and 5 sts at back edge of sleeve and set piece aside. Make another sleeve band the same way, reversing shaping on last row.

Join the pieces, RS*:* When joining the sleeve bands, make sure that the 8 bound-off sts face the front of the garment. Cast on an edge st, k1, work 58 (62, 66, 70) sts in reverse stockinette, k1 = left sleeve, place marker, work 84 (92, 100, 108) sts in stockinette = front, place marker, k1, work 58 (62, 66, 70) sts reverse stockinette, k1 = right sleeve, cast on an edge st = 206 (222, 238, 254) sts total. On all WS rows: work knit over knit and purl over purl.

Raglan shaping: The raglan is shaped on every other row on the front and on every 4th row on the sleeves. The decreases are placed so that there will be a 2-st knit rib flanking each raglan seam.

Decrease row 1, RS: Work up to st after first marker, ssk, work until 2 sts before next marker, k2tog, complete row. Work 1 row.

Decrease row 2, RS: Edge st, ssk, work until 2 sts before first marker, k2tog, slip marker, ssk, work until 2 sts before next marker, k2tog, slip marker, ssk, work until 3 sts remain, k2tog, edge st. Work 1 row.

Repeat these 4 rows.

At the same time, when there are 4 rows of reverse stockinette after the garter stitch edge, place a gusset motif centered on each sleeve.

Work the 4 decrease rows as described above a total of 8 times. There should now be 52 (60, 68, 76) sts on the front between the markers.

On the next pattern row, place the center 22 (24, 26, 28) sts of the front on a holder and work each side separately. Work in short rows from the back edge: work to the neck edge; turn and work back. Now work each row from the back edge with 4 fewer sts each time. *At the same time,* continue to shape raglan as before as long as possible. Continue this way until no more sts can be worked into raglan shaping; the last turn will have 3–7 sts.

Back

Cast on 74 (82, 90, 98) sts and knit 7 rows in garter st. Now continue in stockinette for 46 rows (= same length as gusset on front); place a thread or locking ring marker at each side to make finishing easier. Work 6 rows.

Now place a marker on each side of the center 30 (32, 34, 36) sts and increase as follows: Edge st, k2, LLI, work until 1 st before the first marker, RLI, k2, LLI, work until 1 st before the second marker, RLI, k2, LLI, work until 3 sts remain and end with RLI, edge st = 4 sts increased across row. Repeat this increase row on every 6th row another 4 times = 94 (102, 110, 118) sts. When piece measures 13¾ (14¼, 14½, 15) in / 35 (36, 37, 38) cm, shape armhole by binding off 5 sts at each

side = 84 (92, 100, 108) sts remain.

Now begin shaping raglan: Edge st, ssk, work until 3 sts remain, k2tog, edge st. Decrease the same way on every other row until there are the same number of rows as in back edge of sleeve. Bind off temporarily.

Finishing

Block pieces. Sew the back raglan seams. *Neckband:* Beginning at left raglan seam, pick up all the sts around the neck (undo bound-off sts at back neck). Knit 7 rows in garter st, decreasing the edge sts at the back raglan seams on the first row. Bind off.

Sew side seams. Seam sleeve bands and sew down at underarms. Seam short ends of neckband.

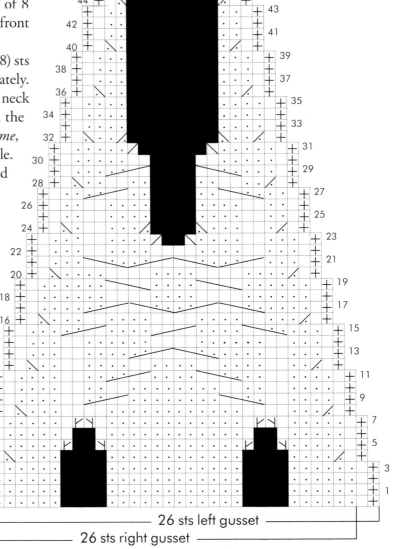

26 sts left gusset

26 sts right gusset

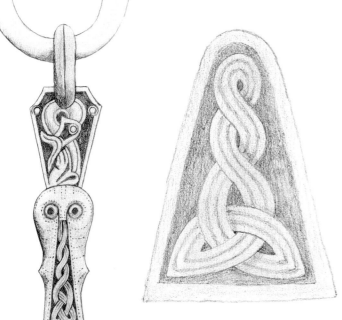

Left: *Bridle detail from Gotland, Sweden*
Above: *Decor on a building detail, Farfa, Italy*

Threeknot Elongated

16 sts (24 sts)

One of the loops of the Threeknot is sometimes elongated and twisted to form a short cable, as on the depicted bridle detail from Gotland, Sweden, shown here on the left. To the right of it, an adornment on a building in Farfa, Italy.

Elisif

Elisif is actually a Viking age version of my name, or rather of Elisabeth; in origin a Hebrew name meaning God's Promise. I can live with that. The Elisif in the history books was a Norwegian queen in the early 11th century. I can live with that too.

To me, this jacket is the essence of femininity in both shape and detail. The triquetras in the gussets have an extra twist, in my symbolic interpretation a way to lift the spirit a bit. So Elisif should both raise your spirit and make you feel like a queen. When you knit it or when you wear it? Both, I hope.

Sizes   S (M, L, XL)

Finished measurements

Chest	34¾ (38¼, 41¾, 45¼) in
	88 (97, 106, 115) cm
Length	22¾ (23¾, 24½, 25¼) in
	58 (60, 62, 64) cm

Materials

Yarn	Silky Wool (p. 14)
Yarn amounts	350 (400, 450, 500) g
Needles	US size 6 / 4 mm
	Cable needle
Notions	7 buttons, ⅝–¾ in / 15–18 mm diameter

Gauge   22 sts × 30 rows in stockinette
                  = 4 × 4 in / 10 × 10 cm

Adjust needle size to obtain correct gauge if necessary.

Edge stitches The outermost st at each side is an edge st. Edge sts are included in the stitch counts and are always knitted unless otherwise specified.

Note Work gusset decreases on the WS by joining the 2 outermost sts of the gusset: work k2tog at the beginning and ssk at the end of the gusset so that the gusset stitches gradually disappear. Otherwise, decrease on RS, inside edge stitches (p. 184).

Chart Gusset with Extended Threeknot, p. 107.

Back

Cast on 143 (153, 163, 173) sts and knit 7 rows, beginning on WS. *On the next row, RS, set up gussets:* Edge st, work 21 (25, 27, 31) sts in stockinette, 32 sts following chart Row 1, 35 (37, 43, 45) sts stockinette, 32 sts of chart Row 1, 21 (25, 27, 31) sts in stockinette, edge st. Continue as set until charted gusset rows are complete; the piece should now be 8¾ in / 22 cm long and 83 (93, 103, 113) sts remain. Continue working the 2 purl sts remaining from each gusset in reverse stockinette with the rest of the row in stockinette. Work 10 (12, 14, 16) rows after completing gussets and then increase as follows: Edge st, RLI, work to and including the first purl rib, RLI, work to second purl rib, LLI, work to edge st, LLI, edge st = 4 sts increased. Increase the same way on every 10th row another 3 times = 99 (109, 119, 129) sts. Now increase on every 10th row but only *between* the purl ribs, another 4 times (this moves the ribs outwards towards the armholes).

At the same time, when piece measures 15 (15½, 15¾, 16¼) in / 38 (39, 40, 41) cm, shape armholes by first binding off 4 (5, 6, 7) sts at each side and then bind off 2 sts at each side 2 times and, finally, decrease 1 st at each side (inside edge sts) on every other row 6 (8, 10, 12) times = 79 (83, 87, 91) sts remain.

When armhole measures 8 (8¼, 8¾, 9) in / 20 (21, 22, 23) cm, bind off the center 31 (31, 33, 33) sts and work each side

separately. Shape shoulders with short rows, beginning at neck edge: bind off 2 sts at neck edge and then work until 7 (8, 8, 9) sts remain; turn and work back. Work 7 (8, 8, 9) sts; turn and work back. Bind off 22 (24, 25, 27) sts for shoulder.

Left front

Cast on 70 (76, 80, 86) sts and knit 7 rows, beginning on WS. *On the next row (RS), set up gusset (the beginning of the row is the side):* Edge st, work 21 (25, 27, 31) sts in stockinette, 32 sts following chart, 15 (17, 19, 21) sts in stockinette, edge st. When the gussets are complete, the piece should be 8¾ in / 22 cm long and 40 (46, 50, 56) sts remain. Continue working the 2 purl sts remaining from the gusset as reverse stockinette, with the rest of the row in stockinette.

After completing gusset, work 10 (12, 14, 16) rows and then increase as follows: Edge st, RLI, work to and including the purl rib, RLI, complete row = 2 sts increased. Increase the same way on every 10th row another 3 times and then increase on every 10th row only *after* the rib (towards the front) another 4 times.

At the same time, when piece measures 15 (15½, 15¾, 16¼) in / 38 (39, 40, 41) cm, shape armhole by first binding off 4 (5, 6, 7) sts at side and then bind off 2 sts at side 2 times and, finally, decrease 1 st (inside edge sts) on every other row 6 (8, 10, 12) times.

Note *At the same time* as working the 4th armhole decrease row, begin shaping the neck with ssk inside the edge st on, alternately, every other and every 4th row 16 (17, 17, 18) times.

When armhole measures 8 (8¼, 8¾, 9) in / 20 (21, 22, 23) cm, shape shoulder with short rows, beginning at neck edge: Work until 7 (8, 8, 9) sts remain; turn and work back. Work (7, 8, 8, 9) sts; turn and work back. Bind off 22 (24, 25, 27) sts for shoulder.

Right front

Work as for left front, reversing shaping, increasing with LLI, and decreasing at the neck with k2tog.

Sleeves

Cast on 46 (48, 50, 52) sts and knit 7 rows beginning on WS. *Next row:* Edge st, work 21 (22, 23, 24) sts in stockinette, p2, work 21 (22, 23, 24) sts in stockinette, edge st. The 2 purl sts at the center continue in reverse stockinette all the way up the sleeve. After working for ¾ in / 2 cm, begin increasing 1 st (inside edge st) at each side on every 6th row 17 (18, 19, 20) times until there are 80 (84, 88, 92) sts total. When the sleeve is 15¾ in / 40 cm long, shape sleeve cap by first binding off 4 (5, 6, 7) sts at each side and then 2 sts at each side. Next, decrease 1 st (inside edge sts) at each side on every other row until 42 sts remain. Bind off 2 sts at the beginning of every row 8 times. Bind off remaining 26 sts.

Finishing

Block pieces. You need to block in two stages, first the top part then the peplum part.

Left Front Band: Pick up and knit 2 sts for every 3 rows along left front = approx 126 (130, 134, 138) sts. Knit 7 rows and then bind off. Mark spacing for 7 buttons with the top one ⅜ in / 1 cm below the first neck decrease and the others spaced below about 2 in / 5 cm apart.

Undo bound-off sts and join right shoulders with three-needle bind-off.

Right Front Band: Pick up and knit the same number of sts along right front as for left front and then pick up and knit sts along back neck: approx 126 (130, 134, 138) + 41 (41, 43, 43) sts = 167 (171, 177, 181) sts. Work as for left front band, but, on the 3rd row, make buttonholes spaced as for buttons. For each buttonhole, bind off 2 sts and then cast on 2 new sts over the gap on the next row.

Undo bound-off sts and join left shoulders with three-needle bind-off. Seam the short ends of front/neck bands.

Seam sides and sleeves. Attach sleeves. Sew on buttons.

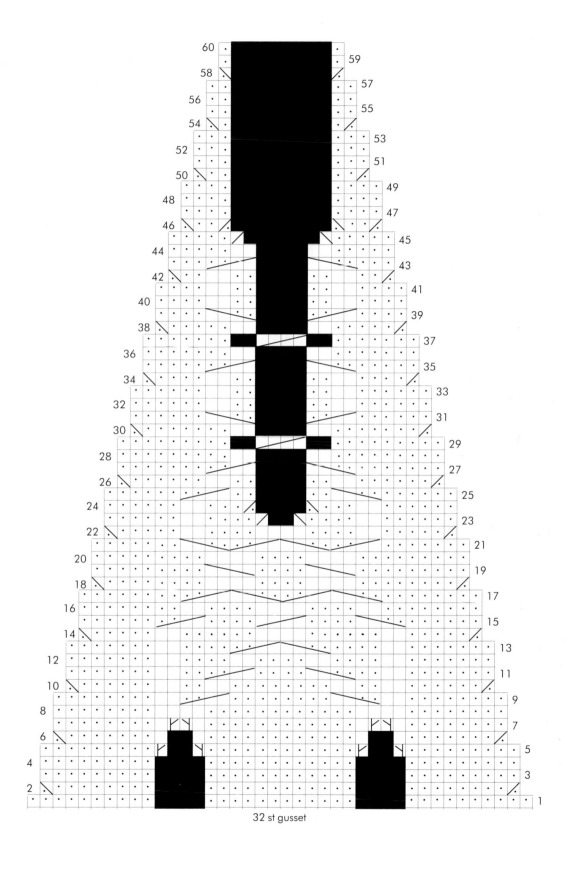

32 st gusset

Threeknot Base Upwards

Threeknot Base Downwards

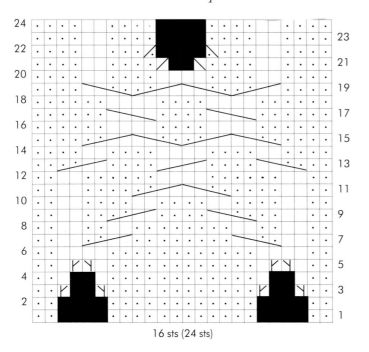

16 sts (24 sts)

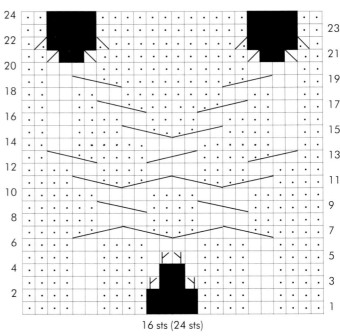

16 sts (24 sts)

If you open up the top loop of an Upwards Threeknot, it becomes obvious that the bottom part, the base, is an Overhand Knot turned the "wrong way". The Downwards Threeknot can of course be used to create the same variation. The only knitted orientation of this pattern that can be achieved is for the bands of the opened loop to extend vertically, which is why it's placed in this chapter rather than in the Overhand Knot chapter. This base can be used to construct other patterns; combining an Upwards and Downwards Threeknot Base creates a motif used on many Viking age objects. The motif can be interpreted as two overhand knots joined back-to-back, but creates a very different impression when knitted (see p. 116).

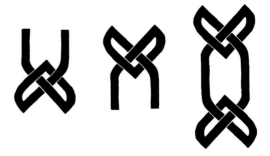

Combined with two Little Knots, this motif can be seen on a sword from Stokke, Norway. Another example from Norway is on a round buckle, where the motif is combined with a trinity symbol. The bronze matrix from Slagelse, Denmark, is another example, and to complete the Nordic trinity, the photo shows a picture stone from Sweden, which, however, predates the Viking age by a couple of hundred years.

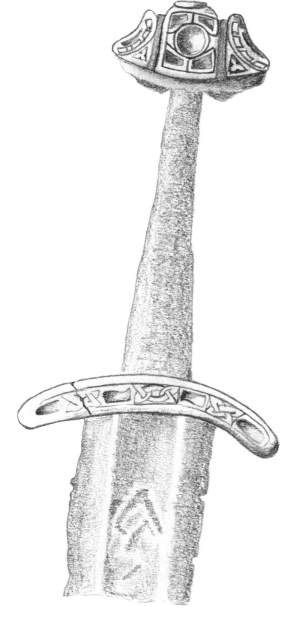

Above: Sword from Stokke, Norway
Top right: Bronze matrix, Slagelse, Denmark
Right: Picture stone, Hellvi, Gotland, Sweden, now at the Historical Museum, Stockholm, Sweden

FYRUNGA

If you look at the drawing of the Fyrunga cross on the next spread, it's pretty obvious where the inspiration for this decorative pillow came from. The pillow has been part of the Knitting along the Viking Trail *exhibition since 1999, when it was hosted by the Gothenburg City Museum on the Swedish west coast. This was the logical "birth place", just 70 miles from Fyrunga where the silver treasure that included the cross was discovered in 1951.*

Recreating the ornamentation was something of a challenge. It didn't take me long to realize that the only way to accomplish the square cross shape would be to knit from the sides and inwards. But what about the middle, where the arms meet in a way that isn't possible to knit? Should I cheat, and leave the middle section empty? Oh no, not this lady! When it dawned on me that I didn't have to stick to just one approach, the problem was solved: Separately knitted I-cords allowed for the bands to continue and overlap neatly in the center.

Finished measurements
Silky Wool   13 × 13 in / 33 × 33 cm
Silky Wool XL 17¼ × 17¼ in / 44 × 44 cm

Materials
Yarn (p. 14)
Small pillow: Silky Wool 150 g
Large pillow: Silky Wool XL 200 g
Needles
Silky Wool   24 and 16 in / 60 and 40 cm circulars
A set of 5 dpn US Sizes 6 / 4 mm
Cable needle
Silky Wool XL 32 and 16 in / 80 and 40 cm circulars
A set of 5 dpn US sizes 8 / 5 mm
Cable needle
Notions Fabric for the back of the pillow, the same measurements as knitted pillow top + seam allowance; pillow form.

Gauge
Silky Wool   24 sts × 34 rows in stockinette st on needles
US 6 / 4 mm = 4 × 4 in / 10 × 10 cm
Silky Wool XL 18 sts × 26 rows in stockinette st on needles
US 8 / 5 mm = 4 × 4 in / 10 × 10 cm
Adjust needle sizes to obtain gauge if necessary.

Note The pillow top is worked in the round, beginning at the outer edges and in towards the center.

Chart Threeknot Base Upwards, see p. 108.

Cast on 320 sts and join to work in the round, being careful not to twist cast-on row. Knit the 1st round, placing a marker at each corner (= 80 sts for each of the 4 sides of the pillow). Continue in purl, with k2 on each side of the center 24 sts in each section. *At the same time*, begin decreasing on each side of every marker with p2tog before and after each marker = 8 sts decreased (when the knit ribs meet, decrease them with ssk before and k2tog after each marker). * Decrease this way for 2 consecutive rounds and work 1 round without decreasing. Repeat from *. After 2½ in / 6 cm, work charted pattern at the center of each section (between the knit ribs). After completing motif, continue with knit over knit and purl over purl. When the knit ribs from the cable pattern meet at each corner, place those sts on a holder. Continue over the purl sts only, decreasing as before until 8 sts remain. Cut yarn and draw through remaining sts.
Working one cord at a time, pick up the knit sts remaining from one cable: Cast on 1 st, work I-cord with 3 sts until cord reaches the opposite set of knit sts. Repeat the I-cord

on every other band. Braid the cords as shown in the photo and join with Kitchener st.

Finishing

Block piece. Steam press the seam allowances under on the fabric for the pillow backing so that the piece is slightly smaller than the knitted pillow top (this will make the pillow puff up better). Sew knitted pillow top onto fabric by stitching into every st of the first round that was knitted on RS. Seam three of the sides. Insert pillow form and seam the last side. Try to make all the stitches the same size. Now make an I-cord to edge the pillow: knit the cord long enough to go around the 4 sides + 2–4 in / 5–10 cm for the loops at each corner. Attach the cord as invisibly as possible.

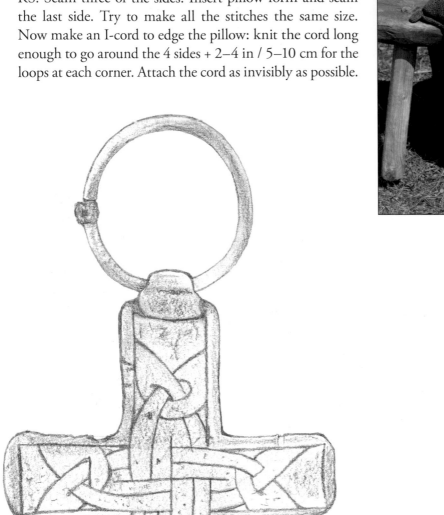

If you break down the details, this cross, found in the Fyrunga plains in Västergötland, Sweden, consists of a Little Knot with Overhand Knots attached. From a knitter's perspective, it still belongs to the Threeknot group of patterns. Cross shaped ornaments, constructed with overhand knots, or variations of such knots, are common in England.

Overhand Knot

An Overhand Knot is one of the basic building blocks in many Viking and Celtic patterns. The symbolism is simple and transparent enough: You create contacts, you tie in with other people, and you tie friendship bands. In English, "tying the knot" is a common euphemism for getting married, and a similar expression exists in Swedish. To tie yourself in knots is not unheard of, but on the other hand, luckily, anything that is tied can also be untied.

Two different perspectives can be applied to an Overhand Knot in terms of how it's made up. One is to cut the bands of a Three Band Braid (see p. 153) at strategic points; the other is to simply tie a single band into a knot. Pull the band through one more time and you have made a Double Overhand Knot. Keep pulling the band through to make a Triple Overhand Knot, a Multiple Overhand Knot and eventually, a Three Band Braid as the vignette illustrates.

I'm particularly fond of the Double Overhand Knot. Frequently, e.g. when opening the *Knitting Along the Viking Trail* exhibition, I tell the story of how the Vikings taught me to tie a knot that doesn't slip. Previously, when I needed to hang something using a nylon fishing line, I always had to burn the knot to keep it from slipping. In working with Viking patterns suitable for knitting, I discovered the Double Overhand Knot, and decided to use it the next time I wanted to hang something. And lo and behold, the knot didn't slip!

Above right: Kirk Andreas Cross 128, Isle of Man, Great Britain
Right: Stone frieze from the cathedral in Pula, Croatia

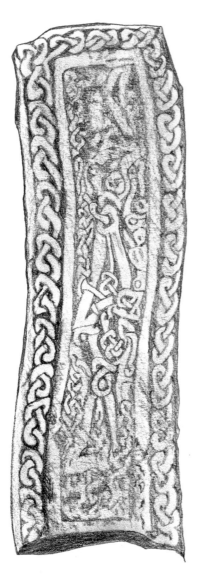

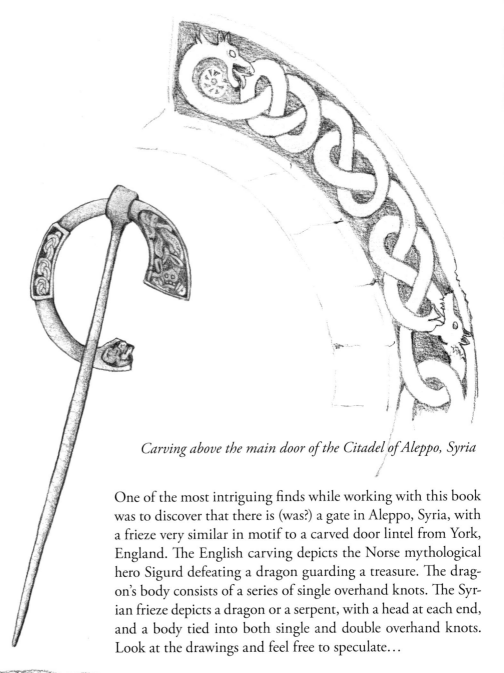

Carving above the main door of the Citadel of Aleppo, Syria

Above: Mount from Vörå, Finland
Right: Pennanular brooch found in Norway

One of the most intriguing finds while working with this book was to discover that there is (was?) a gate in Aleppo, Syria, with a frieze very similar in motif to a carved door lintel from York, England. The English carving depicts the Norse mythological hero Sigurd defeating a dragon guarding a treasure. The dragon's body consists of a series of single overhand knots. The Syrian frieze depicts a dragon or a serpent, with a head at each end, and a body tied into both single and double overhand knots. Look at the drawings and feel free to speculate…

Sigurd Fafnersbane, stone slab, York, England

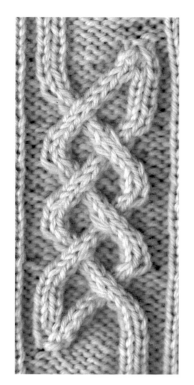

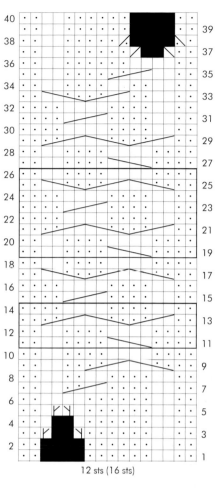

12 sts (16 sts)

Multiple Overhand Knots Left & Right

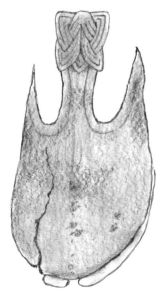

Viking age shoe, Ireland

Two mirrored Overhand Knots back to back form a beautiful panel, as on the depicted mount from Bornholm, Denmark. The same basic pattern, but with the middle bands cut and joined, appears as an isolated motif on a Viking age shoe from Ireland.

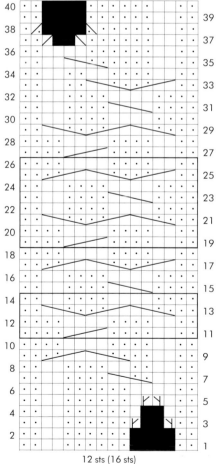

12 sts (16 sts)

Mount from Bornholm, Denmark

Overhand Knot on Bands

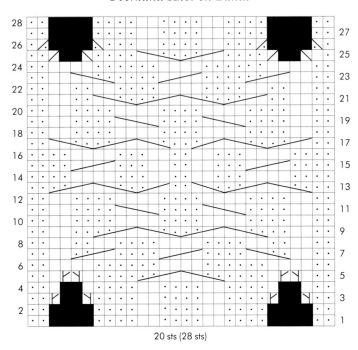

20 sts (28 sts)

Overhand Knot Motif

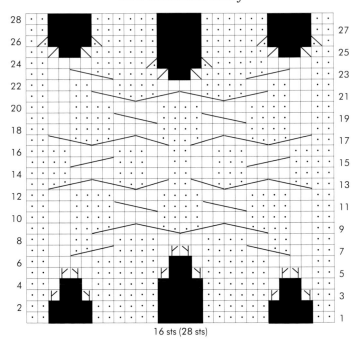

16 sts (28 sts)

On a page from an 11th century manuscript from Dalby, Sweden, hence named *Dalbyboken* (The Dalby Book), I discovered a beautiful Overhand Knot based motif, but with added complexity. I later found the same knot on a church wall in Gotland, Sweden. Similar ornaments are abundant in Irish manuscripts, and related designs can be found in Islamic art. Depicted, an example from Hripsime, Armenia: A decorated window portal. Yet another can be seen on the façade of the church in Tatev (image on p. 162).

Left: Central décor on a window portal in Hripsime, Armenia
Below: Page from Dalbyboken, an 11th century illuminated manuscript found in Dalby, Denmark (Danish at the time, presently Sweden)

Detail of initial "L" with overhand knots on bands from a French Book of Gospels

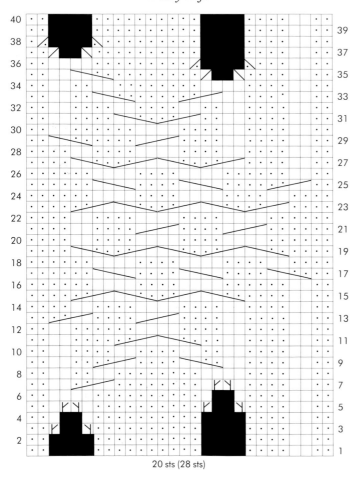

Dalby Left

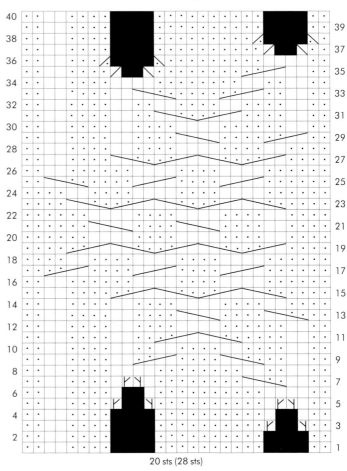

Dalby Right

20 sts (28 sts)

20 sts (28 sts)

Dalby Up & Down

20 sts (32sts to 24 sts)

Detail from an illustration in a Spanish 11ᵗʰ century antiphonary, a copy of an even older one. Antiphonaries contain notations for call and response style of singing.

KATA

Kata means glad, cheerful, and what's not to be glad about? The starting point for this design was a sketch for a pretty summer top with decorative mirrored motifs front and back (rear view on the next spread). Then I decided to split the front to make a sister design: a very wearable vest. Both garments can be dressed up or down as you please.

If I had known that our model would be bringing her dog to the photo session, I might have designed a dog's version as well—it's been known to happen with other designs. As it is, you'll have to settle for the choice of two versions and two yarns; the red vest is made in Silky Wool, the blue top in Hempathy, but any combination is possible.

Sizes   S (M, L, XL)

Finished measurements
Chest   33 (36¼, 39½, 43¼) in
          84 (92, 100, 110) cm
Length   21¾ (22½, 23¼, 24) in
          55 (57, 59, 61) cm

Materials
Yarn   Silky Wool or Hempathy (p. 14)
Yarn amounts
Silky Wool 200 (250, 250, 300) g or
Hempathy 200 (250, 250, 300) g
Needles   US sizes 4 and 6 / 3.5 and 4 for Silky Wool
                  US Sizes 2–3 and 4 / 3 and 3.5 for Hempathy
                  Cable needle
Notions   7 buttons ⅝–¾ in / 15–18 mm

Gauge   22 sts × 30 rows in stockinette on larger
                  needles = 4 × 4 in / 10 × 10 cm
Adjust needle size to obtain correct gauge if necessary.

Edge stitches The outermost st at each side is an edge st. Edge sts are included in the stitch counts and are always knitted unless otherwise specified.

Note Increase on RS with LLI before and RLI after a rib and decrease on WS inside edge sts (at the side and at V-neck, decreases will be inside the knit rib) with k2tog at the beginning and ssk at the end of a row.

Charts Dalby Left & Right, p. 118.

Back
With smaller needles, cast on 96 (104, 112, 120) sts and work the next and subsequent 3 WS rows as follows: Edge st, p1, k43 (47, 51, 55), p2, k2, p2, k43 (47, 51, 55), p1, edge st. On the RS, knit across except for the center 6 sts which are worked in ribbing with knit over knit and purl over purl. This means that the edging is worked in garter except for the two 2-st knit ribs at the center and the 1-st knit ribs at the sides.

Work a total of 7 rows as set and then change to larger needles. Work in reverse stockinette over the sts previously worked in garter st; the center 6 sts and the 2 sts at each side continue as set.

When piece measures 2¾ in / 7 cm, begin decreasing on WS: Edge st, p1, *k2tog, work as set until 4 sts remain and end ssk, p1, edge st. Decrease the same way on every 6th row 5 times = 86 (94, 102, 110) sts. When piece measures 4¼ (4¼, 5¼, 5¼) in / 11 (11, 13, 13) cm, work the Right motif

attached to the first center rib and the Left motif attached to the second center rib.

When piece measures 7 (7½, 8, 8¼) in / 18 (19, 20, 21) cm, increase 1 st inside the knit rib at each side on every 8th row 5 times = 96 (104, 112, 120) sts.

When piece measures 13 (13½, 13¾, 14¼) in / 33 (34, 35, 36) cm, shape armhole by first binding off 5 sts at each side. Next, decrease 1 st inside edge st at each side on every other row a total of 10 (11, 12, 13) times = 66 (72, 78, 84) sts remain. Continue without further shaping until armhole measures 7 (7½, 8, 8¼) in / 18 (19, 20, 21) cm.

Place the center 32 (32, 34, 34) sts on a holder and work each side separately. Bind off 2 sts at neck edge 2 times. The armhole should now measure 8 (8¼, 8¾, 9) in / 20 (21, 22, 23) cm. Shape shoulder with short rows, beginning at neck edge: bind off 1 st, work until 5 (7, 9, 10) sts remain; turn and work back. Bind off remaining 12 (15) 17 (20) sts for shoulder. Work the other side the same way, reversing shaping.

Front

Work as for back to armhole. Divide the piece at the center and work each side separately. Shape the armholes and V-neck at the same time. Shape the armhole as for the back. To shape V-neck, decrease 1 st inside the knit rib on every other row 18 (18, 19, 19) times. Work as set until armhole measures 7½ (8, 8¼, 8¾) in / 19 (20, 21, 22) cm. When at same length, shape shoulder as for back:
Work until 5 (7, 9, 10) sts remain; turn and work back. Bind off 12 (15, 17, 20) sts for the shoulder.
There should now be 3 sts remaining for front band. Cast on a new edge st at the shoulder and continue the band as set until it reaches the center back neck. Bind off. Work the other side the same way, reversing shaping.

Vest, left front

With smaller needles, cast on 48 (52, 56, 60) sts and work the next and following 3 WS rows as:
Edge st, p2, k43 (47, 51, 55), p1, edge st. On RS rows, work knit over knit and purl over purl. After completing 7 rows, change to larger needles and work in reverse stockinette over the 43 (47, 51, 55) sts previously worked in garter st; the 3 sts at front edge and the 2 sts on each side continue as set.

When piece measures 2¾ in / 7 cm, begin decreasing on WS: work until 4 sts remain and end ssk, p1, edge st. Decrease the same way on every 6th row 5 times = 43 (47, 51, 55) sts. When piece measures 4¼ (4¼, 5¼, 5¼) in / 11 (11, 13, 13) cm, work the Dalby Left motif attached to the front rib. When piece measures 7 (7½, 8, 8¼) in / 18 (19, 20, 21) cm, increase 1 st after the knit rib at the side on every 6th row 5 times. When piece measures 13 (13½, 13¾, 14¼) in / 33 (34, 35, 36) cm, shape armhole at the side and V-neck at the same time. Shape armhole by first binding off 5 sts at the side, then decrease 1 st on every other row a total of 10 (11, 12, 13) times. Shape V-neck by decreasing 1 st inside the knit rib on every other row 18 (18, 19, 19) times. Continue until armhole measures 7½ (8, 8¼, 8¾) in / 19 (20, 21, 22) cm. When at same length as back, shape shoulder with short rows, beginning at neck edge: work until 5 (7, 9, 10) sts remain; turn and work back. Using a separate strand of yarn, bind off 12 (15, 17, 20) sts for the shoulder. There should now be 3 sts remaining for front band. Cast on a new edge st at the shoulder and continue the band as set until it reaches the center back neck. Bind off.

Vest, right front

Work as for left front, reversing shaping (decrease at the neck with ssk inside the rib and increase with LLI before the rib). Work the Dalby Right motif attached to the front rib.

Finishing

Block pieces. Undo bound-off sts and join the shoulders with three-needle bind-off.

Top, left neckband: With smaller needles and beginning at the base of the V-neck, pick up and knit 70 (73, 78, 81) sts along left front edge and neck. Work in garter stitch, decreasing 1 st at the *beginning* of every RS row (center front). Knit a total of 5 rows and bind off.

Top, right neckband: Beginning at the center back neck, pick up and knit sts, and work as for left neckband, but decrease at the *end* of every RS row. Sew down band at center front.

Vest, left front band: With smaller needles, pick up and knit 130 (146, 154, 160) sts along left front edge and neck. Knit 5 rows and then bind off. Mark spacing for 7 buttons, with the top one immediately below the base of V-neck and the bottom one ¾ in / 2 cm from cast-on edge; space the rest evenly between.

Vest, right front band: Work as for left front band, but, on row 4, make buttonholes spaced as for buttons. For each buttonhole, k2tog, yo, ssk. The yarnover should be aligned with the button on opposite band. On the next row, k1, p1 into each yarnover. Sew on buttons.

Seam short ends of bands and attach to back neck.

Armhole bands: With smaller needles, pick up and knit 89 (93, 97, 101) sts along armhole and knit 5 rows. Bind off.

Sew side seams and seam short ends of armhole bands.

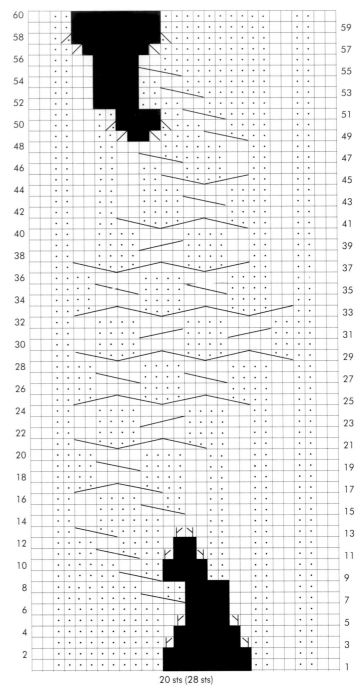

20 sts (28 sts)

Trondheim Left

In my research I have encountered an incredible amount of pattern possibilities. During the early days of the Viking Knits Project I found this pattern, but until now I haven't had a good forum for publishing a charted version. I know I

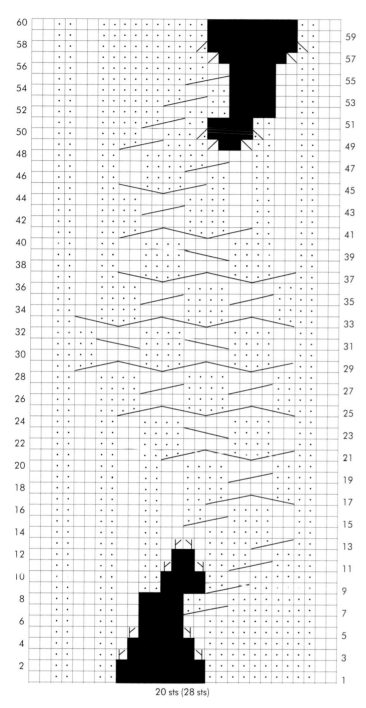

20 sts (28 sts)

Trondheim Right

took it off of an artifact from Trondheim, Norway, because of the name I gave it back then, but I haven't been able to find that artifact again. But here is the knitted variety, a pattern with plenty of decorative potential.

S-hook

While S-shaped and mirrored S-shaped decorations, along with the almost endless variations that this simple shape allows for, were obviously appreciated by the Vikings, their fondness of the S-hook is shared all over the globe. You can find examples of its ornamental use in most cultures, as isolated motifs or in various intertwined and/or meandering forms.

When used as a single decorative element, the S and its mirrored twin are most often assumed to represent a serpent, and this opens up a small universe of possible symbolic interpretations. The serpent is commonly associated with evil, but also with wisdom, sometimes even as a symbol of the enlightened self. Crawling belly down on the ground, the serpent embodies our lowest desires, but at the same time, by shedding its skin, it is also linked to processes of rejuvenation and renewal.

In most cultures, the serpent stands for female energy; the passive and the unpredictable. For some reason, the serpent in Norse mythology is basically genderless, and there are examples of associations to both male and female beings.

However, the single S-shape doesn't appear very often on Viking age objects. I found it on an exceptionally beautiful picture stone from Gotland, which is also where this pretty needle with its double S has its origin. And it can be knitted, both as S and Z-shaped (swatches and charts on the next page).

It also exists in a pointed variety, exemplified by this buckle from Sorø, Denmark, equally attractive as a knitting pattern.

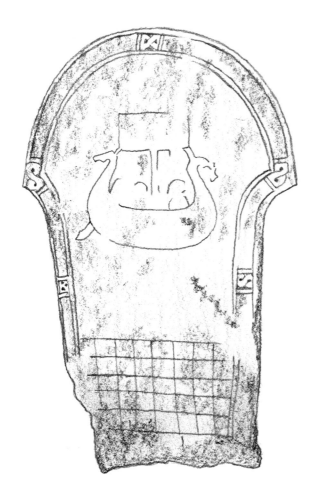

Far left: Picture stone from Gotland, Sweden
Middle: Needle from Gotland, Sweden
Above: Buckle from Sorø, Denmark

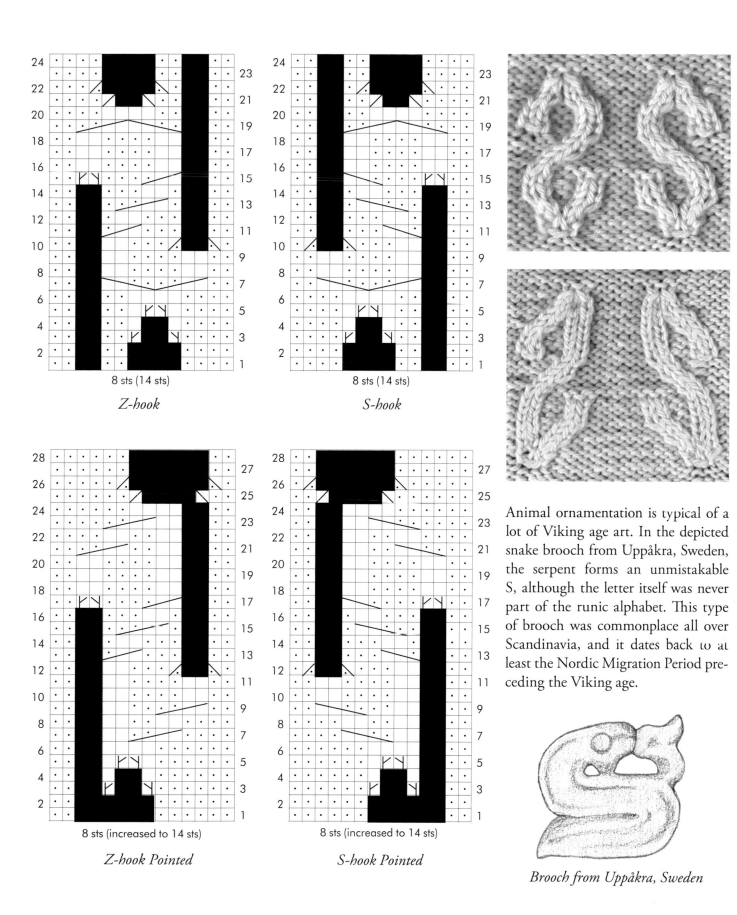

Z-hook

8 sts (14 sts)

S-hook

8 sts (14 sts)

Z-hook Pointed

8 sts (increased to 14 sts)

S-hook Pointed

8 sts (increased to 14 sts)

Animal ornamentation is typical of a lot of Viking age art. In the depicted snake brooch from Uppåkra, Sweden, the serpent forms an unmistakable S, although the letter itself was never part of the runic alphabet. This type of brooch was commonplace all over Scandinavia, and it dates back to at least the Nordic Migration Period preceding the Viking age.

Brooch from Uppåkra, Sweden

Similar brooches were in use by various Germanic tribes, among them the Langobards. This S shape can also be seen in the spiral ornamentation of the Celts, and can in fact be traced all the way back to Mediterranean cultures from thousands of years ago.

But the use of the S-shape as a decorative element extends way beyond Europe, and I have had a lot of fun tracing it in various online historical archives and databases. Among the oldest, although somewhat more angular than in most of the European designs, is a Scythian buckle from the 11th century BC. A similar decoration appears on an Egyptian sock, probably from the 12th century AD, and the S shape was very commonly used in Islamic embroidery from about the same time. It is also hard to imagine an oriental rug, be it Azerbaijani, Kurdish, Persian or Iraqi, without S-shaped pattern elements, oftentimes surrounded by a hexagon.

Travel across the Atlantic, and you will find the S-shape on e.g. the *Vase of the Seven Gods,* depicting parts of the mythology of the Maya Indians, but also on the characteristic pottery of the Peruvian Moche culture.

In northern South America, descendants of escaped African slaves in the Saramaccan tribe in Suriname developed their own decorative style, where interlace is one element. In the depicted "food paddle", the S-shape is used.

The (probably) North African oil lamp with its abundance of pure and simple S-ornamentation was very much

Oil lamp, Rabat, Malta

an unexpected "stumble upon" object. It was displayed in the *Domvs Romana* (Roman House) in Rabat, Malta; a museum Anders and I visited mainly to check out Roman mosaics, some of them with interlace borders.

There are many more, not quite as ancient but frequently equally unexpected, decorative uses of the S shape; examples that I have found intriguing when they surfaced in my research: A 19th century beaded garment from Sarawak in Indonesia, and a Menominee Indian beadwork from around 1850. The poncho worn by Clint Eastwood in the classic Spaghetti Western movie *A Fistful of Dollars* displays a modern interpretation of an ancient S-based pattern. Other examples of contemporary uses of age-old S-shaped design elements can be found on Estonian mittens, certain fabrics from India and in South American woven ribbons. The list could go on and on.

The idea for a meandering S-hook may have begun with the spiral; another universally acclaimed shape, in many cultures associated with spirituality and mysticism. Twin spirals, turning inwards and then outwards again in a repeated pattern, could very well be the origin from which the meandering S-hook emerged.

Spiral shaped ornamentation is frequent in traditional Maori arts and crafts, and the depicted early 19th century *Wakahuia,* a carved wooden treasure box, has a very distinct, somewhat extended, S-hook meander decorating the side. S-hook meanders are also common in Polynesia.

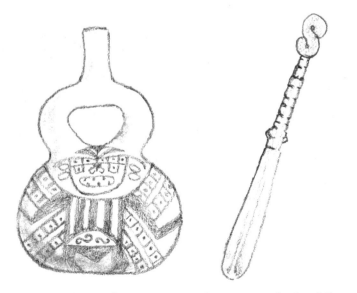

Moche vessel, Peru   Saramaccan food paddle

Both the Vikings and the Celts typically use this motif in a 2-band pattern, where the S in one band hooks into the diagonal part of the other band, as shown in the sketch.

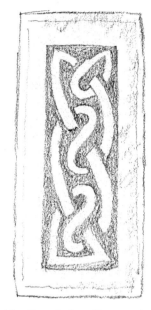

Buckle, Bornholm, Denmark

Mount, Vendel, Sweden

Multiply the basic pattern element and you end up with an S-hook panel, as can be seen on the above buckle from Bornholm, Denmark, and on the incredibly complex Viking age mount from Vendel, Sweden. It is tempting to lose yourself in the myriad of shapes in the center, but it's the border that is relevant for this chapter. This type of border ornamentation is also one of the most frequent adornments in Irish manuscripts and on other objects from the insular culture, where you also find it in more elaborate forms.

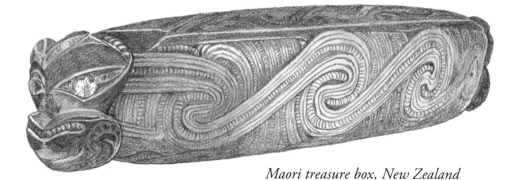

Maori treasure box, New Zealand

Copy of a Langobardic S-shaped brooch, on display in Museo Archeologico Nazionale di Cividale del Friuli, Italy

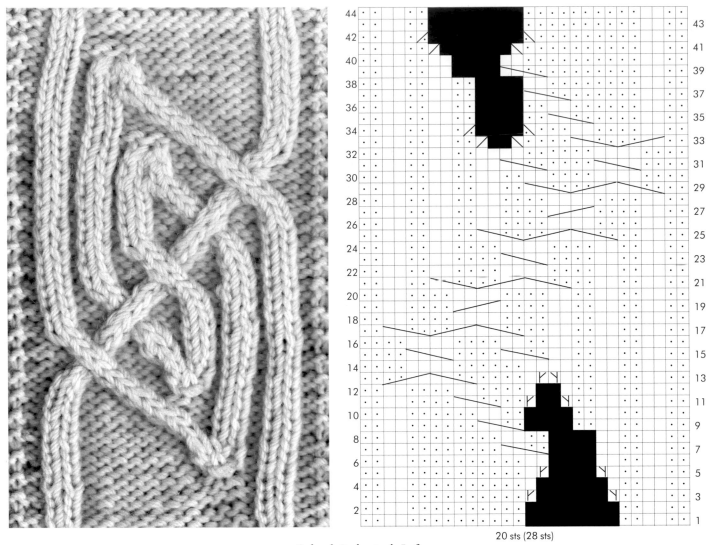

S-hook Labyrinth Left

20 sts (28 sts)

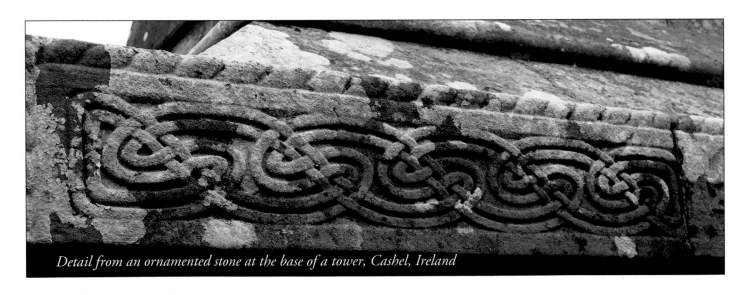

Detail from an ornamented stone at the base of a tower, Cashel, Ireland

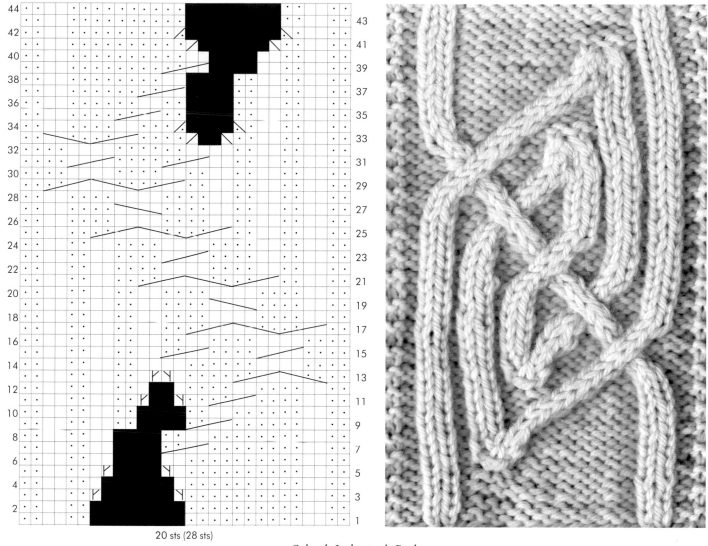

20 sts (28 sts)

S-hook Labyrinth Right

In the above charted examples, the S resides inside a labyrinth that follows the shape of the S; a type of adornment that is predominantly used in Irish illuminated manuscripts. The stone here to the left is actually a part of a small tower at the famous fortress *The Rock of Cashel* in Ireland. It displays a similar pattern, not labyrinthine, but consisting of two parallel S-hooks forming a border.

The "sitting duck" (if I may be so irreverent, it is in fact a dove), contains an example that I found in the famous ornamental masterpiece *The Book of Kells* from around 800 A.D. The bird is sitting on a line of these labyrinthine S-hooks. Such an intriguing design naturally had to be transformed into a knitting pattern and used in a garment.

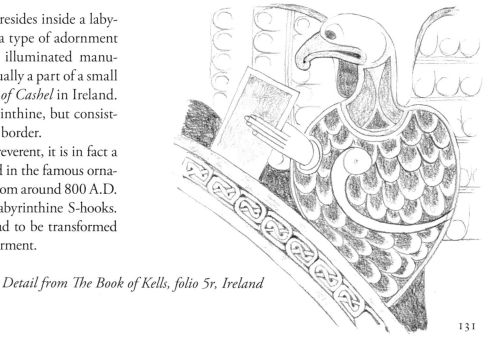

Detail from The Book of Kells, folio 5r, Ireland

Arnhild

The labyrinth S-hook pattern I chose for this design is often used in Irish illuminated manuscripts. It is so dramatic in itself that using it as an all-over pattern was out of the question. Instead, I placed the mirrored versions on the front and back to give the illusion of an added V-neck line. Consequently, the motifs on the arms are placed to give the impression of guarding the hands.

The name Arnhild consists of the words arn, meaning eagle, and hild, meaning fight or battle. Wearing an "eagle in fight" sweater should make you feel invincible, but if not, just enjoy the beauty of it.

Sizes S (M, L, XL)

Finished measurements

Chest	37 (40¼, 43, 45¾) in
	94 (102, 109, 116) cm
Length	21¾ (22½, 23¼, 24) in
	55 (57, 59, 61) cm

Materials

Yarn	Silky Wool (p. 14)
Yarn amounts	300 (350 400 450) g
Needles	US size 6 / 4 mm
	16 in / 40 cm circular for neckband
	Cable needle
Gauge	22 sts × 32 rows in stockinette st
	= 4 × 4 in / 10 × 10 cm

Adjust needle size to obtain correct gauge if necessary.

Edge stitches The outermost st at each side is an edge st. Edge sts are included in the stitch counts and are always knitted unless otherwise specified.

Note Always work the st immediately inside the edge st at each side (along the sides and sleeves up to the armhole/ sleeve cap) in stockinette. On RS, work k2 at the beginning and end of the row. This will form a knit rib when the side seams and sleeves are joined. Increase inside these 2 sts.

Charts S-hook Labyrinth Left, p. 130 and Right, p. 131, and Transition Charts Left and Right, p. 134.

Back

Cast on 106 (114, 122, 130) sts and set up pattern.

Setup row, WS: Edge st, p1, (k2, p2) 3 (4, 5, 6) times [= 14 (18, 22, 26) sts ribbing], * k12, p2, (k2, p2) 2 times (= 10 sts ribbing); repeat from * 3 times and end row with another 4 (8, 12, 16) sts ribbing. There are now 14 (18, 22, 26) sts in ribbing at each side and 3 rib panels of 10 sts with knit sts in between. Work the next 6 rows, with the ribbing as set and the 12 sts in between the ribs in garter st (knit every row). Next, work the 12 sts between the rib sections in reverse stockinette st.

When work measures 9¾ (10¾, 11½, 12¼) in / 25 (27, 29, 31) cm, work the charted motifs centered across the piece. Work the right motif before the center and the left motif after. There will be a knit rib between the motifs. Begin by working Rows 1–8 and then Rows 9–36 of the basic charts. Work the Transition following charts A, right and B, left and then Rows 9–36 once more. Finish with Rows 37–44 of the basic chart.

At the same time, when piece measures 12¾ (13, 13½, 13¾) in/ 32 (33, 34, 35) cm, shape armhole by binding off first 5 sts at each side, then 2 sts 0 (1) 1 (2) times. Next, decrease 1 st at each side on every other row 6 (8) 9 (10) times = 84 (84, 92, 92) sts remain (there should be 1 knit rib left inside each edge st).

Chart A

Chart B

After completing charted rows, work knit over knit and purl over purl for the rest of the piece.

When armhole measures 8¼ (8¾, 9, 9½) in / 21 (22, 23, 24) cm, place the center 28 (28, 32, 32) sts on a holder and work each side separately. Shape shoulder with short rows, beginning at neck edge: Bind off 2 sts, work until 9 (9, 10, 10) sts remain; turn and work back. Work 9 (9, 10, 10) sts; turn and work back. Bind off 26 (26, 28, 28) sts for shoulder. Work the other side the same way, reversing shaping.

Front

Work as for back until beginning the final chart; the armhole should measure 6 (6¼, 6¾, 7) in / 15 (16, 17, 18) cm. Place the center 22 (22, 26, 26) sts on a holder for the neck and work each side separately. Shape neck by decreasing 1 st at neck edge on every other row 5 times. When armhole measures 8 (8 ¼, 8 ¾, 9) in / 20 (21 22 23) cm, shape shoulder with short rows, beginning at neck edge: Work until 9 (9, 10, 10) sts remain; turn and work back. Work 9 (9, 10, 10) sts; turn and work back. Bind off 26 (26, 28, 28) sts for shoulder. Work the other side to match, reversing shaping.

Sleeves

Cast on 54 (54, 62, 62) sts and set up pattern.

Setup row, WS: P2, (k2, p2) 2 (2, 3, 3) times [= 10 (10, 14, 14) sts ribbing], k12, p2,(k2, p2) 2 (2, 3, 3) times [= 10 sts ribbing], k12, p2,(k2, p2) 2 (2, 3, 3) times [= 10 (10, 14, 14) sts ribbing]. There should now be 10 (10, 14, 14) sts ribbing at each side and 1 rib panel of 10 sts at the center with knit sts in between.

On the next 6 rows, continue the ribbing as set and work the 12 sts in between the ribs in garter st. After the 7 rows of edging, work the 12 sts between the ribs in reverse stockinette st.

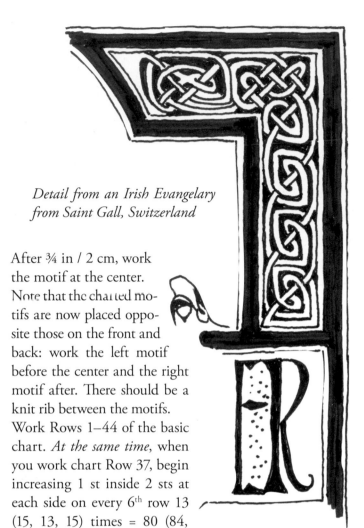

Detail from an Irish Evangelary from Saint Gall, Switzerland

After ¾ in / 2 cm, work the motif at the center. Note that the charted motifs are now placed opposite those on the front and back: work the left motif before the center and the right motif after. There should be a knit rib between the motifs. Work Rows 1–44 of the basic chart. *At the same time*, when you work chart Row 37, begin increasing 1 st inside 2 sts at each side on every 6th row 13 (15, 13, 15) times = 80 (84, 88, 92) sts. Work new sts in ribbing.

After completing charted rows, work knit over knit and purl over purl for the rest of the sleeve.

Sleeve Cap: When sleeve is 16½ in / 42 cm long, bind off 5 sts at each side to begin shaping sleeve cap. Next, decrease 1 st at each side on every other row until 32 sts remain. Bind off 2 sts at the beginning of every row 8 times. Bind off remaining 16 sts.

Finishing

Block pieces. Undo bound-off sts and join shoulders with three-needle bind-off.

Neckband: Beginning at the center front, pick up and knit 100 sts around the neck. Begin on RS (= WS of collar) and work back and forth: Edge st, *p2, k2; repeat from * across and end with p2, edge st. Continue in k2, p2 rib as set for 6¼ in / 16 cm. Bind off in ribbing.

Sew side and sleeve seams. Attach sleeves.

An appealing variation will become the result if you place the S inside a Figure Eight and allow the cut ends of both shapes to join. A mirrored version is also possible to knit, and equally attractive, so I swatched and charted it too. A pointed, and thereby more directional, version is not difficult to make, see the Bjärs motif, p. 74–75.

S-hook Motif Left

S-hook Motif Right

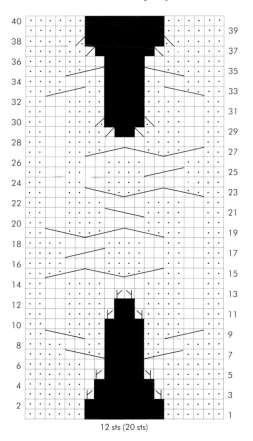

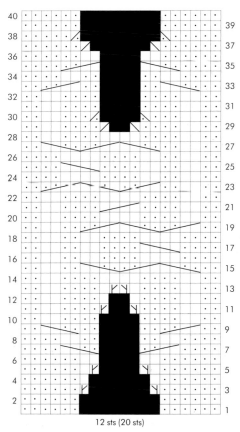

12 sts (20 sts)

12 sts (20 sts)

hofvarpnir

Hofvarpnir literally means "he who throws his hoofs around" and was the name of the horse of the goddess Gná. Gná was an asynja in the circle of the goddess Frigg. Call on her when you want to send an urgent message, or use these socks to get your own feet flying.

I first spotted the type of shoes in the photo in a store window in Bornholm, a Danish Baltic Sea island. The storefront displayed a totally irresistible sign: "Handmade shoes and guitars". Over the years I have bought many pairs of this model shoes, and with great restraint, Anders has managed to keep his guitar purchases down to two.

Sizes Women's (Men's)

Materials
Yarn Silky Wool (p. 14)
Yarn amounts 100 (150) g
Needles US size 2–3 / 3 mm
Set of 5 dpn US size 2–3 / 3 mm
Cable needle

Gauge 24 sts in stockinette = 4 in / 10 cm
Adjust needle size to obtain correct gauge if necessary.

Chart S-hook Motif Left and S-hook Motif Right, p. 135, and Chart A.

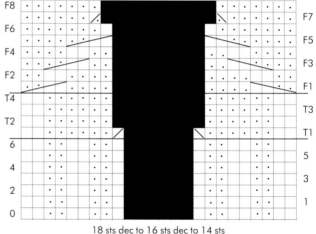

18 sts dec to 16 sts dec to 14 sts

Chart A

Right sock
Leg: With straight needles, cast on 58 (66) sts and work back and forth, beginning on WS: (P2, k2) 5 (6) times, work 18 sts following chart A, Row 0, (k2, p2) 5 (6) times. Continue, working the 20 (24) sts at each side in ribbing as set and the center 18 sts following the chart. Work sts as set 5 (7) times for ribbing and then transition row T1 one time, 2 sts decreased = 56 (64) sts.
Now work sts as set for 3 more rows, then work following the chart for the S-hook Motif Right, Rows 1–38 (there are now 22 (26) sts in ribbing on each side of the chart's 12 sts) and end with Rows F1–F8 of chart A where 2 sts are decreased = 54 (62) sts. The leg should now be 6¾ (8) in / 17 (20) cm long. Bind off the edge st at each side = 52

(60) sts remain. Move stitches onto 4 dpn, with 13 (15) sts on each dpn; join to work in the round. Mark beginning of round and knit around in stockinette for 5 rounds.
Heel Flap: Work the heel flap back and forth in stockinette over the sts on dpn 1 and 2 for 18 (22) rows. *Take foot measurements from this point (end of heel flap).*
Heel Turn: Shape heel turn with short rows:
K14 (18) sts, ssk; turn and p3 (7), p2tog; turn
K4 (8), ssk; turn and p5 (9), p2tog; turn
K6 (10), ssk; turn and p7 (11), p2tog turn
Continue the same way until you can't make any more decreases. The last row has 14 (18) sts and ends on WS. Now work in the round over sts on all 4 dpn: Work the 14 (18) sts of heel; pick up and knit 18 (22) sts along side of

heel flap, work across needles 3 and 4 in stockinette; pick up and knit 18 (22) on other side of heel flap = 76 (92) sts total. Divide heel sts evenly between needles 1 and 2. Place marker for beginning of round between needles 4 and 1.

Gusset: On needle 1: ssk, k to end of needle; needle 2: work until 2 sts remain on needle, k2tog, work across needles 3 and 4 in stockinette. Decrease the same way on every round until 13 (15) sts remain on each needle. Continue around in stockinette until foot measures 8 (9) in / 20 (23) cm or desired length.

Toe:

Needle 1: K1, ssk, k10 (12)
Needle 2: K10 (12), k2tog, k1
Needle 3: Work as for needle 1
Needle 4: Work as for needle 2

Decrease the same way on every round until 8 sts remain. Cut yarn and draw through remaining sts.
Seam leg using 1 st as seam allowance.

Left sock
Work as for right sock, working the motif following the chart for S-hook Motif Left.
Work the heel flap with sts on needles 3 and 4. Beginning of round after heel turn is between needles 2 and 3.

Another beautiful Irish variation on the meandering S theme is formed by interlacing regular and mirrored S-hook panels. The sheer beauty of it demanded that I make both a narrow and a wide version.

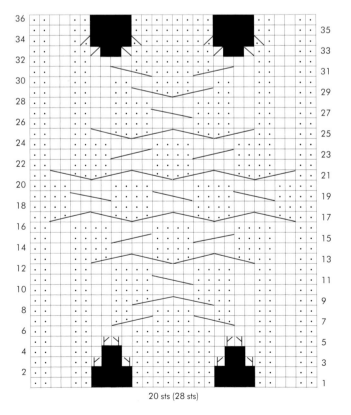

S-hook Interlaced Meander Narrow

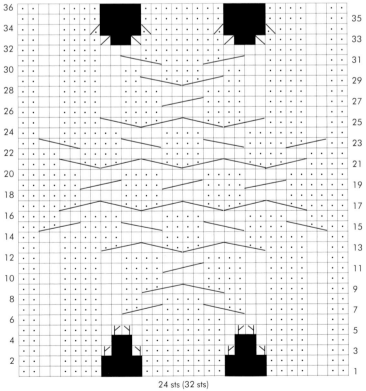

S-hook Interlaced Meander Wide

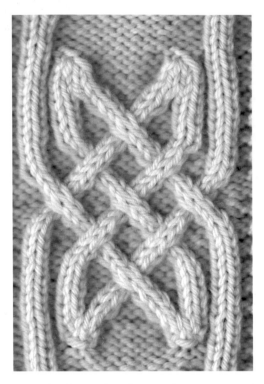

20 sts (28 sts)

24 sts (32 sts)

JARNSAXA

Here's a strong design named after a strong woman in Norse mythology, the giantess Jarnsaxa, who was the mother of Thor's son Magne. She is known as "the one with the iron sword", but that was not the reason for our choice of backdrop in the main photo: a reconstruction of a Viking age smithy. We simply thought they would look good together.

In shape, Jarnsaxa is a classic sweater. However, the placed cable motifs, beautiful interlaced meandering S-hooks, are eye-catching, and the vertical ribs give a body-hugging impression. This adds up to a most distinctive and wearable garment.

Sizes S (M, L, XL)

Finished measurements

Chest 35½ (39½, 43¼, 47¼) in
90 (100, 110, 120) cm

Length 19¾ (20½, 21¼, 22) in
50 (52, 54, 56) cm

Materials

Yarn Silky Wool (p. 14)

Yarn amounts 350 (400, 450, 500) g

Needles US sizes 4 and 6 / 3.5 and 4 mm
16 in / 40 cm circular US size 4 / 3.5 mm
for neckband
Cable needle

Gauge 22 sts × 30 rows in stockinette on larger
needles = 4 × 4 in / 10 × 10 cm

Adjust needle sizes to obtain correct gauge if necessary.

Edge Stitches The outermost st at each side is an edge st. Edge sts are included in the stitch counts and are always knitted unless otherwise specified.

Note 1 st inside the edge st at each side (along the sides and sleeves up to the armhole/sleeve cap) is worked in stockinette. On RS rows, always k2 at the beginning and end of the row. This forms a stockinette rib at each side to use for seaming the sides and sleeves.

Charts S-hook Interlaced Meander Narrow for size S, p. 138, S-hook Interlaced Meander Wide for remaining sizes, p. 138. Sizes S and XL have an extra purl st on each side of the charted sts and the panel is 22 (26) sts instead of 20 and 24 sts as indicated on the chart.

Back

With smaller needles, cast on 102 (110, 122, 134) sts and set up pattern.

Setup row, WS: Edge st, p1, k12 (13, 19, 22), * p2, k3 (2, 2, 3), p2, k12 (16, 16, 16), p2, k3 (2, 2, 3); repeat from * 2 times, p2, k12 (13, 19, 22), p1, edge st.

Row 2: Knit.

Repeat these 2 rows 3 times and then work the setup row once more. There should now be 4 knit ribs on RS. Change to larger needles and continue the stockinette ribs but work reverse stockinette over the sts which were previously in garter st. When piece measures 5½ (6, 6¼, 6¾) in / 14 (15, 16, 17) cm, work Rows 1–36 of the Interwoven S-hook motif centered on back. When motif is complete and piece measures 11 (11¾, 12¾, 13½) in / 28 (30, 32, 34) cm, work the motif again, this time inside the 15 sts at each side so that it aligns with the stockinette ribs.

At the same time as beginning the motifs, shape armholes by first binding off 5 (6, 7, 8) sts at each side. Next bind off 2 sts 0 (0, 2, 3) times at each side. Now begin shaping on WS: K1 (edge st), k2tog, work until 3 sts remain, ssk, k1 (edge st). Decrease the same way on every other row 7 (7, 8, 8) times total = 78 (84, 84, 90) sts remain. When armhole measures 8 (8¼, 8¾, 9) in / 20 (21, 22, 23) cm, place the center 24 sts on a holder and work each side separately. Shape shoulder with short rows, beginning at neck edge: Bind off 3 sts and work until 8 (9, 9, 10) sts remain; turn and work back. Work 8 (9, 9, 10) sts; turn and work back. Bind off remaining 24 (27, 27, 30) sts for shoulder. Work other shoulder the same way, reversing shaping.

Front

Work as for back until armhole measures 5½ (6, 6½, 6¾) in / 14 (15, 16, 17) cm. Place the center 16 sts on a holder and work each side separately. At neck edge, decrease 1 st inside edge st on every other row 7 times. When armhole measures 8 (8¼, 8¾, 9) in / 20 (21, 22, 23) cm, shape shoulder with short rows, beginning at neck edge. Work until 8 (9, 9, 10) sts remain; turn and work back. Work 8 (9, 9, 10) sts; turn and work back. Bind off remaining 24 (27, 27, 30) sts for shoulder. Work other side the same way, reversing shaping.

Sleeves

With smaller needles, cast on 50 (54, 54, 58) sts and set up pattern.

Setup row, WS: Edge st, p1, k10 (11, 11, 12), p2, k3 (2, 2, 3), p2, k12 (16, 16, 16), p2, k3 (2, 2, 3), p2, k10 (11, 11, 12), p1, edge st.

Row 2: Knit.

Repeat these 2 rows 3 times and then work the setup row once more. There should now be 4 knit ribs on RS. Change to larger needles and continue the stockinette ribs but work in reverse stockinette over the sts previously in garter st. Shape sleeve by increasing 1 st inside the stockinette rib at each side on every 10th (10th, 8th, 8th) row 12 (12, 15, 15) times = 74 (78, 84, 88) sts. *At the same time,* when sleeve is 4¾ in / 12 cm long, work an Interwoven S-hook motif centered on the sleeve so it aligns with the stockinette ribs. When the sleeve is 16½ in / 42 cm long, shape sleeve cap by binding off 5 (6, 7, 8) sts at each side. Now decrease 1 st inside edge st at each side on every other row until 32 sts remain. Bind off 2 sts at the beginning of every row 8 times and then bind off remaining 16 sts.

Finishing

Block pieces. Undo bound-off sts and join shoulders with three-needle bind-off.

Mock Turtleneck: With smaller circular, pick up and knit 88 sts around the neck. Join and work around in k2, p2 ribbing for 3½ in / 9 cm (align the stockinette ribs at back and front). Bind off in ribbing. *Alternate Round Neck:* Pick up and knit sts as for Mock Turtleneck but work back and forth in garter st, except for the stockinette ribs which continue as set. Knit 7 rows (4 ridges) and then bind off. Sew sleeve and side seams. Attach sleeves.

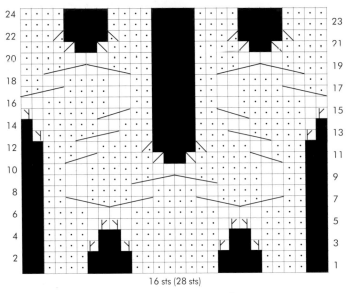

S-hook Horizontal Border

16 sts (28 sts)

Above a type of horizontal S-hook border that I have so far only found in Islamic cultures, where it's frequently used decorating walls and household items.

Another pattern that is very common in Islamic cultures is formed by interlacing S- and Z-hooks horizontally. I discovered it on a 15th century stone relief framing a door opening in Kayseri, Turkey (not shown), but I have found the same basic design on an Egyptian mosque lamp, and on a Swedish Viking age fibula of unknown origin, but possibly from Gotland just like so many other Viking age objects (shown on the next spread). After I had swatched it, I decided that it had all the merits to be included in a garment as well. (Disa, p. 145) Note the fact that where the ends are closed, they form Twisted Wing Loops (see p. 26–27).

Above top: Detail of decorative stone panel in Konya, Turkey
Above bottom: Corner decoration on a 9th century, possibly Merovingian, evangelary from France

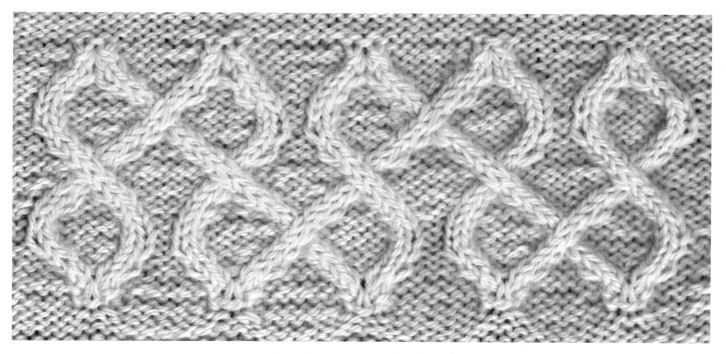

S-hook Horizontal Interlaced Border

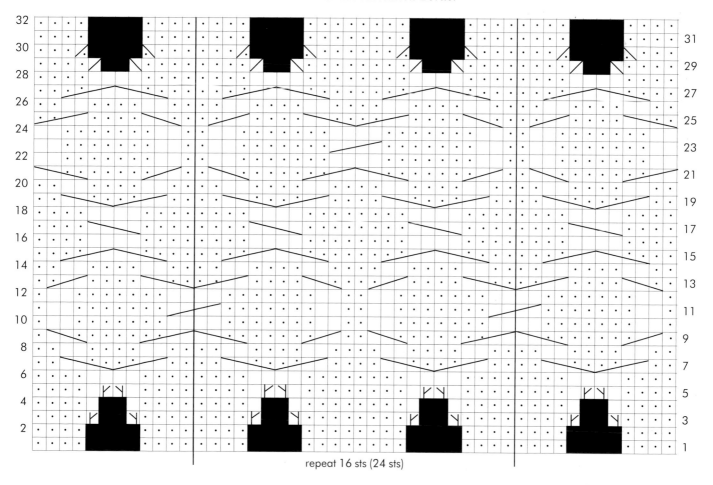

repeat 16 sts (24 sts)

The chart on the previous spread shows the entire panel including the endings. If you knit just the repeat, you end up with the Down motif; if you knit the sections before and after the repeat, the Up motif is created.

S-hook Horizontal Motif Down

S-hook Horizontal Motif Up

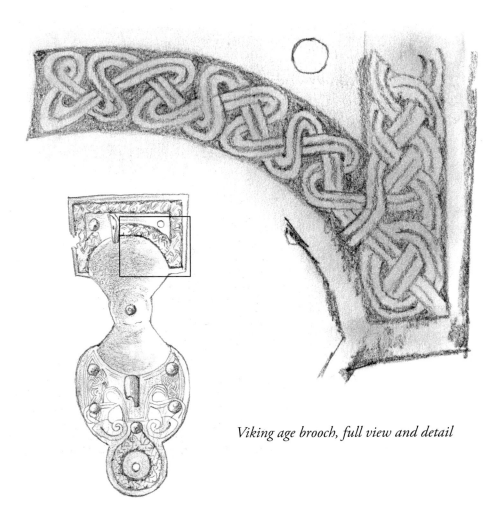

Viking age brooch, full view and detail

Ðisa

In Norse mythology, a dís is a spirit associated with fate. Dísir may act as protective spirits but are not necessarily benevolent. My Disa is a cardigan with a border and motif of interlaced S-hooks, patterns that are found on Viking objects as well as on Islamic ones.

When Anders spotted our cute young model at a folk music festival and approached her parents, he had no idea that her father had made one of my designs for himself, with a related motif and in a similar color. It certainly is a small world.

Sizes 4 (6, 8, 10) years

Finished measurements
  Chest 23¾ (25¼, 26¾, 28¼) in
         60 (64, 68, 72) cm
  Length 18¼ (19¾, 22, 25¼) in
          46 (50, 56, 64) cm

Materials
Yarn Silky Wool (p. 14)
Yarn amounts 200 (250, 300, 300) g
Needles 32 in / 80 cm circulars US sizes 4 and 6 / 3.5 and 4 mm
  Cable needle
Notions 13–15 buttons ⅜–½ in / 10–12 mm diameter

Gauge 22 sts × 32 rows in stockinette on larger needles = 4 × 4 in / 10 × 10 cm
Adjust needle sizes to obtain correct gauge if necessary.

Edge stitches The outermost st at each side is an edge st. Edge sts are included in the stitch counts and are always knitted unless otherwise specified.

Note The cardigan is worked back and forth in one piece up to the armholes. The piece is divided at the armholes and then the front and back are each worked separately.

Charts S-hook Horizontal Interlaced Border, p. 143. For S-hook Horizontal Motif Down, see explanation on p. 144.

Body

With smaller needles, cast on 258 (274, 290, 306) sts and knit 7 rows in garter st. Change to larger needles and work 6 rows in reverse stockinette. Work the border and then continue in reverse stockinette until the piece measures 11¾ (13, 14¼, 15½) in / 30 (33, 36, 39) cm. Now, inside the edge sts, work k2tog across = 130 (138, 146, 154) sts. Change back to smaller needles and knit 8 rows in garter st. Change to larger needle again and continue in reverse stockinette. After ¾ in / 2 cm, work a motif inside 5 sts from the front edge at each side. When piece measures 1¼ (1½, 2, 2½) in / 3 (4, 5, 6) cm after the garter st band, continue in reverse stockinette and divide the work for front and back: work 30 (32, 34, 36) sts, bind off 5 sts, work 60 (64, 68, 72) sts, bind off 5 sts, work 30 (32, 34, 36) sts.

Left Front: Shape armhole at the side by decreasing 1 st on every other row 1 (2, 3, 4) times = 29 (30, 31, 32) sts remain. Continue without further shaping until 6 (8, 10, 12) rows past the end of the motif. Place 10 (10, 11, 11) sts at front edge on a holder and then shape neck by decreasing 1 st at neck edge on every other row 5 times. When armhole measures 5¼ (5½, 5, 6¼) in / 13 (14, 15, 16) cm, bind off remaining 14 (15, 15, 16) sts for shoulder.

Right Front: Place right front sts on needle and work as for left front, reversing shaping.

Back: Place back sts on needle and shape armhole by decreasing 1 st at each side on every other row 1 (2, 3, 4) times = 58 (60, 62, 64) sts remain. Continue without further shaping until armhole measures 3½ (4, 4¼, 4¾) in / 9 (10, 11, 12) cm. Place the center 26 (26, 28, 28) sts on a holder and work each side separately. At neck edge, bind off 2 sts. When armhole measures 5¼ (5½, 5, 6¼) in / 13 (14, 15, 16) cm, bind off remaining 14 (15, 15, 16) sts for shoulder. Work the other side the same way, reversing shaping.

Sleeves

With smaller needles, cast on 38 (40, 42, 44) sts and knit 7 rows in garter st. Change to larger needles and work 6 rows in reverse stockinette. Now work the motif centered on the sleeve. *At the same time* as working Row 17 of the chart, begin increasing 1 st at each side every 6th row 10 times = 58 (60, 62, 64) sts. When sleeve is 10¾ (11¾, 13, 14¼) in / 27 (30, 33, 36) cm long, shape sleeve cap by first binding off 3 sts at each side. Next, decrease 1 st at each side on every other row until 22 sts remain. Bind off 3 sts at each side and then bind off remaining 16 sts.

Finishing

Block pieces. Undo bound-off sts and join shoulders with three-needle bind-off.

Neckband: With smaller needles, pick up and knit 72 (74, 78, 80) sts around the neck. Work 7 rows in garter st and then bind off.

Left front band: With smaller needles, pick up and knit 2 sts for every 3 rows along left front edge; pick up and knit 2–3 sts along garter st band. The precise number of sts isn't important, but, the stitches should be picked up evenly along the edge so that it won't pucker. Approx 90 (98, 104, 112) sts should work. Knit 7 rows in garter st and then bind off.

Mark spacing for buttons, with 1 at neck edge, 1 at the garter st band at the waist and 2–3 in between. Evenly space other buttons below as you like.

Right front band: Work as for left front band, but, on row 3, work buttonholes spaced as for buttons. For each buttonhole: yo, k2tog.

Sew sleeve seams and attach sleeves. Sew on buttons.

Decor on an Islamic candle stick

Braiding

Braiding consists of bands running in parallel and at the same time traveling above and below each other vertically and diagonally. The small Viking age tuning peg from Denmark shown below is a quirky example of this, where form rather than function is the determining factor behind the design. We don't know when man started sourcing the decorative potential of braided patterns, but we do know that they have been in use for several thousand years, and I think it's safe to assume that every culture with a need for rope also identified uses beyond the purely practical.

Two bands

A plain two-band pattern is actually a twist rather than a braid. Pushing a rope into soft clay and thus getting a decorative imprint is a practice that has probably been in use since mankind first started making ropes. Some very early examples of this type of ornamentation exist, e.g. on a 5,000 year-old pot found in present day Iran and on 4,000 year-old cylinder-shaped clay stamps from the Middle East (Turkey and Syria). Slightly more "recent" are the numerous mosaics that were abundant in Mediterranean classical antiquity ornamentation.

Below left: Roman mosaic, Santa Giulia Museo, Brescia, Italy
Below middle: Mexican clay stamp
Below right: Tuning peg, Denmark

South America can provide other examples. One of the drawings shows The Smiling God (even if I'd be prone to call him The Snarling God), a Jaguar God depicted on a stone slab in Chavin, Peru, with hair consisting of intertwined serpents. The Chavin culture existed during the major part of the first millennium BC. My other example is a fairly recent discovery of a Mayan stone relief from Yaxuma, Mexico.

Joining the bands at one end creates a loop. An incised glyph from the grave of Nefertari, one of the principal wives of the Egyptian pharaoh Ramses the Great, shows a twist ending in a loop. This is the letter "h" in the Egyptian alphabet, reminiscent of both the Ankh and the Tyet Knot. The Ankh symbolizes Life and is common in Egyptian texts about rebirth. The Christian Egyptian Copts adopted the Ankh as a symbol of the resurrection of Christ, and this symbol later developed into what is now commonly known as the Celtic Cross. The Tyet Knot, also known as the Knot of Isis, is common as an amulet for its alleged protective powers. All three are also closely related to the Minoan Sacral Knot (basically a loop on some kind of cord), and, to further encourage you to speculate, the Minoan Snake Goddess is often portrayed in a manner very close to the woman goddess in the photo of a picture stone from Gotland, Sweden, complete with a two-band twist border ornament.

Mayan stone relief, Yaxuma, Mexico.

Egyptian glypth, Ankh and Tyet Knot

Picture stone, Gotland, Sweden

The Smiling God, Chavin, Peru

As discussed in the Rings & Chains chapter, the ends of a band can be joined to form a ring, and the ring may be twisted. A single twist creates a Figure Eight, or, depending on orientation, an Eternity symbol (see p. 53). But if you keep turning, you create a Two Band Twist which can, theoretically, be made to any length by repeating Rows 9–16.

It didn't take many of thc countless hours I have spent pattern hunting in various archives to conclude that Two Band Twists have global appeal.

My Viking age examples are keys from Gotland, Sweden. Slightly older

is the 6th or 7th century Merovingian Germanic belt buckle found in France, where it is combined with a Fourknot.

Merovingian belt buckle, France

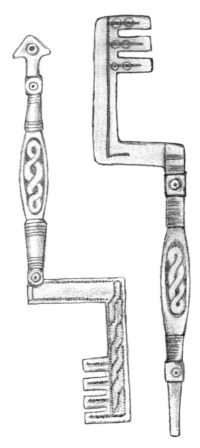

Two Band Twist

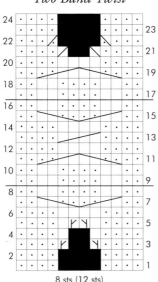

8 sts (12 sts)

Raphia fabric, Shoowa Kuba tribe, Congo

Above left: Viking age keys, Gotland, Sweden
Left: Langobardic belt ornament, displayed in
Museo Archeologico Nazionale di Cividale del Friuli, Italy

"Crutch" capital
Santa Giulia Museo, Brescia, Italy

Iron age pendant, Kumma, Estonia

In Roman mosaics it's abundant, as well as on Roman and Langobardic stone reliefs. Africa provides examples from both Western (Kuba, Yoruba and Hausa) and Eastern (Somalia and Ethiopia) regions. On the below stone from Croatia, two mirrored twists are placed side-by-side. According to some sources I've found, to the Maoris two or more twists of the bands represents interaction between peoples and cultures.

Horse brush handle, Mongolia

Stone fragment, Muzej Lapidarium, Novigrad, Croatia

Three bands

To make a braid according to the strict definition of the word, you need at least three bands, but with an odd number of bands, the endings obviously can't be made by joining two and two together. Both the Vikings and the Celts commonly solved this "problem" by letting the residual band end in a snake figure, or as a loop or spiral.

The Three Band Braid is abundant through history as well as pre-history; e.g. in a Roman mosaic that was recently discovered under the Bank of London, or the one in the photo, from Brescia, Italy, where the Three Band Braid is used framing a motif. It appears on Greek urns as well as in the pattern repertoire of the African Hausa and Yoruba people. Together with a swarm of other interlace ornaments, it appears on a Viking age sword from Ultuna, Sweden (next page), and on several Central and South American objects, among them this metal disc from Guatemala (shown on the right).

Chavín metal disc, Guatemala

Porporo stick, pre-Hispanic, Peru

Below: Roman mosaic, Santa Giulia Museo, Brescia, Italy

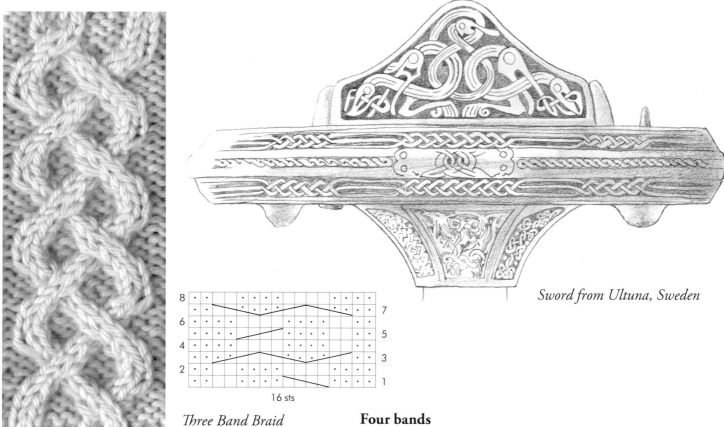

Sword from Ultuna, Sweden

Three Band Braid

16 sts

Langobardic gold crucifix with a Three Band Braid
Museo Archeologico Nazionale di Cividale del Friuli, Italy

Four bands

The cross-cultural popularity of the Four Band Braid may be due to the fact that it is the narrowest symmetrical braid that can be made. Joining the bands two by two creates neat endings.

The bands travel diagonally in 45 degree angles, making this pattern a perfect candidate for creating mitered corners, as can be seen in the depicted 5th century Coptic fabric from Egypt, but perfectly doable in knitting as well.

5th century Coptic fabric, Egypt

The chart shows a pointed beginning (the rows before the first bold line) and a pointed ending (the rows after the second bold line), while the middle section is the repeat for the actual braid. Knitting centered endings and omitting the repeat will create the Little Knot, the smallest four band based isolated motif that can be achieved, but including the repeat section will make any braid length possible.

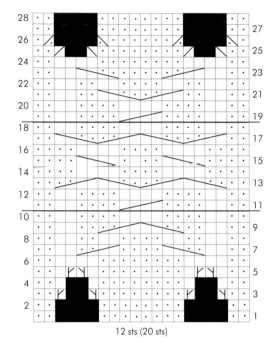

Four Band Braid

12 sts (20 sts)

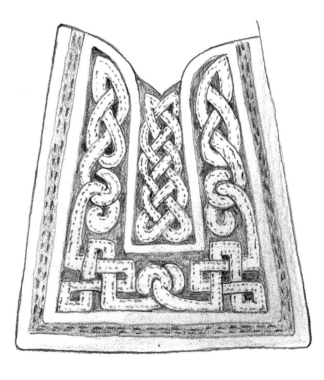

Khalka saddle detail, Mongolia

In the Rings & Chains chapter, I describe a four band pattern where the outer bands are creating a cross woven into the ring that is formed by cutting the crossings of the inner bands (the Ring on Cross panel, p. 45). I showed an isolated motif based on this pattern, but with the outer bands cut and joined as well (the Ring on Cross motif, p. 45). If, instead, you cut the outer band, letting the inner bands create a ring shape through which the cross is woven, you end up with the pattern Cross on Bands below. I haven't found anyone using it in my artifact research, but it is beautiful nevertheless.

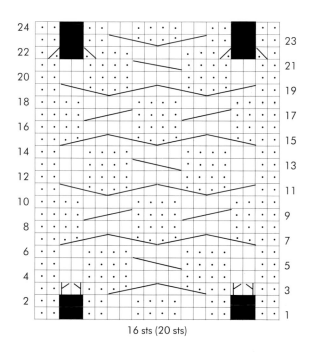

Cross on Bands

16 sts (20 sts)

Octagonal pillar, Santa Giulia Museo, Brescia, Italy

Langlif

I'm not really a fashion designer, although I have to adapt to current trends in things like colors and preferred garment shapes to a certain extent. Instead, I strive to make my designs timeless in the best sense of the word without having them lose their character in the process. I think Langlif is a good example of that design philosophy, hence the name.

Langlif was originally a nickname, "longlife", but I have found a few instances of Langlif as a "real" first name in medieval Norway. In Denmark the form Langliva starts appearing from c. 1150. It's very probable that the place name Langliuetorp in North Yorkshire, England, means "the farmstead of a woman named Langlif". Threads come together...

Sizes S (M, L, XL)

Finished measurements

Chest 35½ (39½, 43¼, 47¼) in
90 (100, 110, 120) cm

Length 22¾ (23½, 24½, 25¼) in
58 (60, 62, 64) cm

Materials

Yarn Favorite Wool (p. 14)

Yarn amounts 500 (550, 600, 650) g

Needles US size 8 / 5 mm
16 in / 40 cm circular US size 7 / 4.5 mm
for neckband
Cable needle

Gauge 17 sts × 24 rows in stockinette on larger
needles = 4 × 4 in / 10 × 10 cm

Adjust needle sizes to obtain correct gauge if necessary.

Edge stitches The outermost st at each side is an edge st. Edge sts are included in the stitch counts and are always knitted unless otherwise specified.

Charts Cross on bands, p. 155, and Transition chart A, (p. 158) which is only worked once. Rows R1 and R2 show the ribbing and rows T1 and T2 show the transition into the pattern—note the increase on row T1. The pattern consists of 40 rows: Rows 3–24 of the chart for the cable

pattern and Rows 1 and 2 which are repeated 9 times for the straight bands.

Back

Cast on 90 (98, 106, 114) sts. Work in k2, p2 ribbing for 1¼ in / 3 cm, beginning on WS with p2, k2. Change to larger size needles and set up pattern.

Setup row, RS: Edge st, k5 (9, 9, 13), * p2, k2, work 14 sts following Chart A Row T1, k2, p2, k6 (6, 10, 10), repeat from * one time, p2, k2, work 14 sts following Chart A Row T1, k2, p2, k5 (9, 9, 13), edge st. 6 sts are increased on Row T1 = 96 (104, 112, 120) sts.

After Rows T1 and T2, start working following the Cross on Bands chart but begin 1st repeat on Row 3.

When piece is 14¼ (14½, 15, 15½) in / 36 (37, 38, 39) cm long, shape armhole at each side. Bind off 3 (4, 5, 6) sts at each side and then decrease 1 st at each side on every other row 4 (5, 6, 7) times = 82 (86, 90, 94) sts. When armhole measures 8 (8¼, 8¾, 9) in / 20 (21, 22, 23) cm, bind off the center 22 sts (26 sts if you are in the part of the pattern with increased sts) and work each side separately. Shape neck and shoulder with short rows, beginning at neck edge: Bind off 4 sts, work until 8 (9, 10, 11) sts remain; turn and work back. Work 8 (9, 10, 11) sts; turn and work back. Bind off remaining 26 (28, 30, 32) sts for shoulder. Work the other side the same way, reversing shaping.

Front

Work as for back until armhole measures 6 (6½, 6¾, 7) in / 15 (16, 17, 18) cm. Place the center 16 sts (20 sts if you

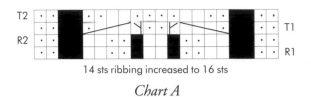

14 sts ribbing increased to 16 sts

Chart A

are in the part of the pattern with increased sts) on a holder and work each side separately. At neck edge, decrease 1 st inside edge st on every other row 7 times. When armhole measures 8 (8¼, 8¾, 9) in / 20 (21, 22, 23) cm, shape shoulder with short rows, beginning at neck edge. Work until 8 (9, 10, 11) sts remain; turn and work back. Work 8 (9, 10, 11) sts; turn and work back. Bind off remaining 26 (28, 30, 32) sts for shoulder. Work other side the same way, reversing shaping.

Sleeves

Cast on 34 (34, 42, 42) sts. Work in k2, p2 ribbing for 1¼ in / 3 cm, beginning on WS with p2, k2. Change to larger needles and set up pattern.

Setup row, RS: Edge st, k5 (5, 9, 9), p2, k2, work 14 sts following Chart A Row T1, k2, p2, k5 (5, 9, 9), edge st. 2 sts are increased on Row T1 = 36 (36, 44, 44) sts.

After Rows T1 and T2, start working following the Cross on Bands chart but begin 1st repeat on Row 3. *At the same time,* when sleeve measures 2 in / 5 cm, shape sleeve by increasing 1 st at each side on every 8th row 11 (13, 11, 13) times = 58 (62, 66, 70) sts. When sleeve is 16½ in / 42 cm long, shape sleeve cap by first binding off 3 (4, 5, 6) sts at each side. Next, decrease 1 st at each side on every other row until 22 sts remain. Bind off 2 sts at the beginning of every row 4 times and then bind off remaining 14 sts.

Finishing

Block pieces. Undo bound-off sts and join shoulders with three-needle bind-off.

Mock Turtleneck: With smaller size circular, pick up and knit 72 sts around the neck. Join and, making sure stockinette ribs are aligned at front and back, work around in k2, p2 ribbing for 3½ in / 9 cm. Bind off in ribbing.
Sew sleeve and side seams. Attach sleeves.

Six bands

Six Band Braids are not nearly as common as their three and four band "cousins". Short versions, sometimes as short as a Large Knot, can be found on Viking and Celtic objects. The chart shows a Six Band Braid with rounded endings. It doesn't have to have endings; knitting just the repeat section works fine. A Large Knot will be the outcome of knitting the entire chart.

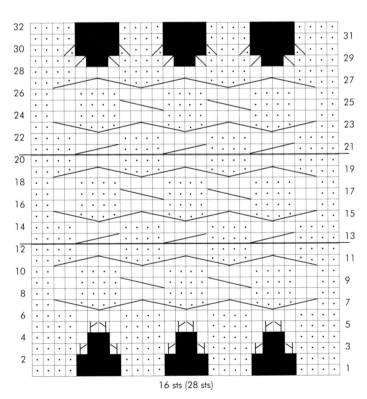

16 sts (28 sts)

Thus, the Large Knot can be perceived as a cut-off section of a Six Band Braid, symmetrical in height and width, where the cut-off bands are joined two by two, but it can also be seen as a basic form of the Little Knot & Ring (see p. 88). This basic form shows up on the Roman mosaic in the photo, placed in an orientation that is unfortunately impossible to knit. The drawing shows an extended version of the Large Knot, decorating a Byzantine buckle from the 6th or 7th century. Passementeries can sometimes have a very similar design as, and may very well have served as inspiration for, Large Knots and Six Band Braids.

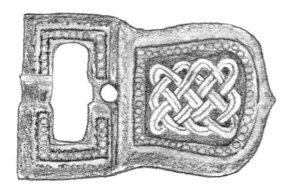

Above: Byzantine style filigree buckle, early 7th century, Cividale del Friuli, Italy
Right: Roman mosaic, The Basilica of Aquileia, Italy

The braids can of course be widened ad infinitum by adding bands, preferably in pairs, to create an all-over lattice pattern. While researching for this book, I was pleasantly surprised to find this portal from an early Italian monastery on display in the Santa Giulia Museum in Brescia, Italy.

Portal from San Salvatore, 6th century, Museo Santa Giulia, Brescia, Italy

The Six Band Braid allows for many types of variations, and is also well suited for making mitered corners. One such "evolution" is the pattern I have named the Hausa knot, from the frequent use the Nigerian Hausa People made of it in their textiles. It can be seen as an extended version of the Eternal Knot (discussed on the next page). It's often used combined with the Little Knot, and is also common in Langobardic ornamentation.

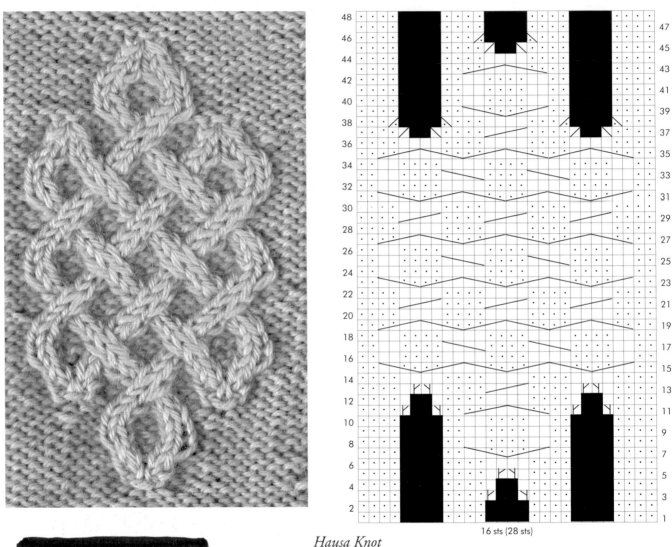

Hausa Knot

Left: Motif from an Ijebu-Ode fabric, Nigeria
Right: Detail of Langobardic stone frieze, Croatia

The Eternal Knot, also known as the Endless Knot, is a Buddhist symbol, one of the Eight Auspicious Symbols. There are almost innumerable meanings attributed to this symbol, but it is commonly regarded as representing Eternity and Wholeness. It's typically shown in a horizontal orientation, but can actually be turned in any direction, including diagonally. In its knitted manifestation, a vertical orientation will yield the most pleasing result.

Detail from Alhambra, 14th century, Spain

In Buddhist culture, the Eternal Knot is commonly used decorating textiles and house exteriors, based on the belief that endless loops will confuse evil spirits and head off their attacks. The knot is also known as the Dragon Knot, since the symbolic representation may have emerged from images of guarding dragons. It stands for the intertwining of wisdom and compassion, but also for opposites joining in harmony, thus having the same symbolic essence as Yin and Yang.

The knot is widespread in Asia. It commonly appears on storage chests and boxes, but I have seen it decorating Mongolian boots, silk fabrics and various household items, and on valuables like the Mongolian pendants shown on p. 83.

It is also abundant in Islamic ornamentation. In Palacio de Leones, Alhambra, Spain, it appears repeatedly on all walls alongside a version of the Fourknot. It can be found with other braided motifs in several ancient Muslim buildings, among them the mausoleum of Ashik Pasha depicted in the Loops chapter. The ornaments on the Sts. Paul and Peter church in Tatev, Armenia, shown on the next spread, also includes the Dalby Knot, discussed in the Overhand Knot chapter. But it was not unheard of in Roman culture either, as the below buckle from Autun, France, shows.

Roman belt buckle, Autun, France

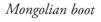
Mongolian boot

*Decoration on the church of St. Paul and Peter,
Tatev, Armenia*

An interesting square version decorates both Gaut's Cross and Sandulf's Cross from the Norse period in Isle of Man, and Gaut's cross actually is named after the Scandinavian craftsman who carved it.

Eternal Knot on a stone from Isle of Man, Great Britain

 Both rounded and pointed versions of the Eternal Knot are charted and swatched here, followed by Skabersjö on Bands (where the central top and bottom loops are opened up). The Skabersjö motif and Skabersjö on Cables (as in the vignette) were discussed in my *Viking Patterns for Knitting* book.

Eternal Knot

16 sts (28 sts)

Skabersjö on Bands, swatch

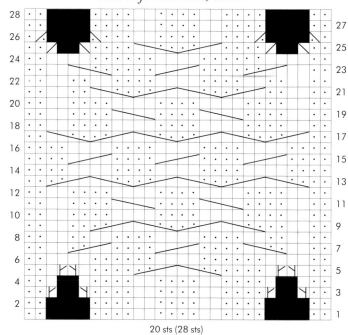

Langobardic frieze, Croatia

Eternal Knot Pointed

Pattern motif on an Anatolian carpet depicted on a 15th century Persian painting

Skabersjö on Bands, chart

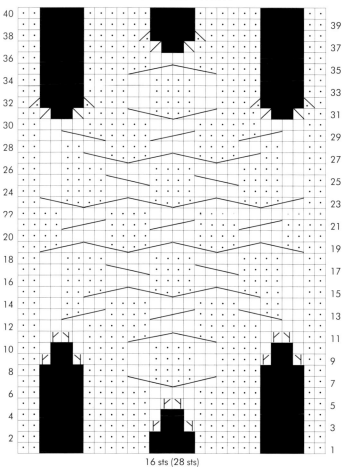

16 sts (28 sts)

20 sts (28 sts)

mist

Mist was a Valkyrie who, together with her sister Rist, served mead from the goat Heidrun to the einherjar, the dead Vikings in Valhalla. Her name means exactly the same as the English word mist.

The vest is an eye catcher with its combination of three pattern elements, the Twisted Loop panels running down the front and back and on the front framing a Hausa Knot. You have a choice of sleeves or an unusual armhole treatment in the same ridge pattern as the collar. If you don't like turtlenecks you could make do with just one ridge. If you choose sleeves, you'll find a downwards pointing loop above the cuffs and in both versions on the back, just below the neck. And to complete the design, a bag with the same Hausa Knot as you find on the front.

Sizes XS (S, M, L, XL, XXL)

Finished measurements

Chest 30¾ (34¾, 38½, 42½, 46½, 50½) in
78 (88, 98, 108, 118, 128) cm

Length 16¼ (16½, 17, 17¼, 17¾, 18¼) in
41 (42, 43, 44, 45, 46) cm

Materials

Yarn Favorite Wool (p. 14)

Yarn amounts

Vest 250 (300, 300, 350, 350, 400) g
Sweater 400 (450, 500, 550, 600, 650) g
Bag 150 g

Needles US sizes 6 and 7 / 4 and 4.5 mm
16 in / 40 cm circular US size 6 / 4 mm
for neckband and edging of bag
Cable needle

Notions for Bag

Handles, a small piece of heavy foam, approx 4 × 11 in / 10 × 28 cm (make sure that the foam fits the bottom of your bag). Lining fabric, approx 17¾ × 27½ in / 45 × 70 cm.

Gauge 18 sts × 26 rows in stockinette on larger
needles = 4 × 4 in / 10 × 10 cm.
Adjust needle sizes to obtain correct gauge if necessary.

Edge stitches The outermost st at each side is an edge st. Edge sts are included in the stitch counts and are always knitted unless otherwise specified.

Charts Twisted Wing Loop Down Left and Right, p. 27; Downwards Pointing Loop, p. 16; Hausa Knot, p. 160.

Welt pattern

Row 1: Knit
Row 2: Purl
Row 3: Knit

Repeat these 3 rows for welt with 3 rows reverse stockinette alternating with 3 rows stockinette.

Back, vest and sweater

With smaller needles, cast on 70 (80, 88, 98, 106, 116) sts and set up pattern:

Row 1, WS: K20 (25, 28, 33, 36, 41), p2, k26 (26, 28, 28, 30, 30), p2, k20 (25, 28, 33, 36, 41)
Row 2: Knit

Repeat these 2 rows 3 times and then work Row 1 once more = 9 rows total.

Change to larger needles and continue, working reverse stockinette over the sts previously worked in garter st. The knit ribs help position the panels: The motif on the Twisted Wing Loop Down Right is placed so that the 2 knit ribs

of the chart are above the first rib and the knit rib of the Twisted Wing Loop Down Left chart is above the second knit rib (see photo).

Repeat Rows 1–24 throughout.

When piece measures 8 in / 20 cm, shape armhole. First bind off 2 (4, 4, 6, 6, 8) sts and then 2 sts at each side 0 (0, 1, 1, 2, 2) times. Next, decrease 1 st at each side on every other row 2 (4, 4, 6, 6, 8) times = 62 (64, 68, 70, 74, 76) sts. When armhole measures 4¾ (4¾, 5¼, 5¼, 5½, 5½) in / 12 (12, 13, 13, 14, 14) cm, work a Downwards Pointing Loop motif centered on the back.

When armhole measures 7½ (8, 8¼, 8¾, 9, 9½) in / 19 (20, 21, 22, 23, 24) cm, shape shoulders with short rows: work until 7 (6, 7, 8, 7, 8) sts remain; turn and work until 7 (6, 7, 8, 7, 8) sts remain. Work each of the next 4 rows 6 (7, 7, 7, 8, 8) sts shorter. Place the remaining 24 (24, 26, 26, 28, 28) sts on a holder for the back neck and, using a separate strand, bind off 19 (20, 21, 22, 23, 24) sts for each shoulder.

Front, vest and sweater

Work as for back until front measures 5½ (5½, 6, 6, 6¼, 6¼) in / 14 (14, 15, 15, 16, 16) cm. Work a Hausa Knot motif centered on the front. After completing charted rows, continue as for the back until the armhole measures 5½ (6, 6¼, 6¾, 7, 7½) in / 14 (15, 16, 17, 18, 19) cm. Place the center 14 (14, 16, 16, 18, 18) sts on a holder for the neck and work each side separately. Bind off 1 st at neck edge on every other row 5 times. When at same length, shape shoulder with short rows as for back, beginning at neck edge: Work until 7 (6, 7, 8, 7, 8) sts remain; turn and work back. Work 6 (7, 7, 7, 8, 8) sts; turn and work back. Bind off 19 (20, 21, 22, 23, 24) sts for shoulder. Work the other side the same way, reversing shaping.

Sleeves, sweater

With smaller needles, cast on 38 (40, 42, 42, 44, 46) sts and * knit 1 row, purl 1 row, knit 1 row; repeat from * (3 rows reverse stockinette alternating with 3 rows stockinette).

Work in welt pattern until there are 5 reverse stockinette welts. Work 1 more stockinette ridge, increasing 6 (6, 6, 8, 8, 8) sts evenly spaced over the last row = 44 (46, 48, 50, 52, 54) sts.

Change to larger needles and reverse stockinette. Increase 1 st at each side on every 10th (8th, 8th, 6th, 6th, 6th) row 7 (7, 8, 8, 9, 9) times = 58 (60, 64, 66, 70, 72) sts.

At the same time, when sleeve is 2¾ in / 7 cm long, work a Downwards Pointing Loop motif centered on the sleeve.

When sleeve is 16½ in / 42 cm long, shape sleeve cap by first binding off 2 (4, 4, 6, 6, 8) sts at each side and then another 0 (0, 2, 2, 2, 2) sts at each side. Next, decrease 1 st at each side on every other row until 32 sts remain. Bind off 2 sts at the beginning of every row 8 times (decreasing 4 times at each side). Bind off remaining 16 sts.

Finishing

Block pieces. Undo bound-off sts and join shoulders with three-needle bind-off, with WS facing WS (so ridge from bind-off will be on the RS).

Collar: With short, smaller size circular, pick up and knit 70–80 sts around the neck and work around in welt pattern, alternating 3 rounds stockinette with 3 rounds reverse stockinette until there are 6 reverse stockinette welts. Bind off knitwise.

Vest, Armhole Bands: With smaller needles, pick up and knit 2 sts for every 3 rows along armhole, approx 87–99 sts. Work in welt pattern, beginning on Row 2 and, *at the same time*, begin short rows. Work until 10 sts past the shoulder seam; turn and work back until 10 sts past shoulder seam. Throughout, work each row with 3 (3, 3, 4, 4, 4) more sts than previous row until there are 12 rows in welt pattern. Now work over all the sts until the reverse stockinette welt is complete. Bind off knitwise on RS.

Sew sleeve and side seams. Attach sleeves on sweater.

Bag

Make front and back alike: With larger needles, cast on 48 sts and work 3 rows in stockinette. Continue in reverse stockinette and increase 2 st at each side on every 10th row 7 times = 62 sts. *At the same time*, when the reverse stockinette section is 2½ in / 6 cm long, work a Hausa Knot motif at the center, following the chart. After completing motif, work in reverse stockinette for another 1¼ in / 3 cm. The piece should now be approx 8 in / 20 cm long. Bind off.

Sides and bottom: With larger needles, cast on 20 sts and purl 1 row = WS. Set up pattern: Edge st, 2 sts stockinette, 14 sts garter st, 2 sts stockinette, edge st. Continue as set until piece is 27 in / 68 cm long. Bind off.

Finishing: Block pieces. Cut out lining fabric following shaping and size of bag + seam allowances. Seam lining. Sew the sides and bottom to the front and back pieces of bag.

Edging: With smaller size circular, pick up and knit 48 sts along the front, 14 sts along side, 48 sts along back, and 14 sts along the other side = 124 sts total. Join and work around in reverse stockinette for 5 rounds. Bind off.

Sew down lining below the edging. Sew on handles securely.

Closely related to the Skabersjö motif is the Braided Hearts motif. It is a unicursal hexagram. One interpretation is that it represents the fusion of opposites. It can be drawn as a hand sign and is thus sometimes used that way in mystic rituals. In some pagan beliefs it symbolizes extensive self-awareness and the quest for high spiritual goals. As a symbol of dedication to the Divine Rulers, it is believed to be a component of both Greek and Hindu mythology.

The Yourubas generally attribute traits like continuity and balance to braided patterns. Braided Hearts on a crown can symbolize the chain of Holy Forefathers linked all the way back to Oduduwa, the first man.

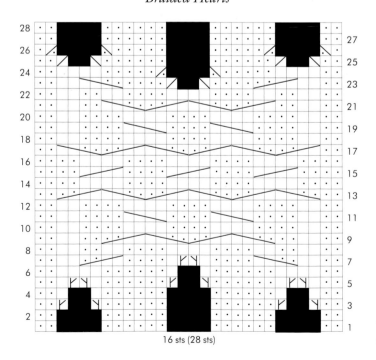

Braided Hearts

16 sts (28 sts)

Top: Langobardic building detail, Split, Croatia
Middle: Scandinavian type tortoise shaped buckle, England
Bottom: Bronze buckle, Sigtuna, Sweden

Fragment of a parapet on display at the Museo Archeologico Nazionale di Cividale del Friuli, Italy

unn

According to the etymologists, the name Unn has a component of generosity and love, so I tried to make this design a generous one that the whole family can love to wear. It's the only unisex design in the book, and even though we haven't photographed it on a female model, just pick an appropriate size and shorten the sleeves, and you have a very attractive woman's sweater.

The combination of an easy, comfortable shape, a flattering collar and a distinctive Braided Hearts motif just above the heart makes this a perfect his and hers combo in the heavier yarn. In a thinner yarn it becomes an adorable garment for the little ones (see next spread).

Sizes   XS (S, M, L, XL, XXL)

Finished measurements

Chest   38½ (42½, 43¼, 47¼, 53½, 57½) in
98 (108, 110, 120, 136, 146) cm

Length   26 (26½, 26¾, 27¼, 27½, 28) in
66 (67, 68, 69, 70, 71) cm

Materials
Yarn   Silky Wool XL (p. 14)
Yarn amounts   550 (600, 650, 700, 750, 800) g
Needles

US sizes 7 and 8 / 4.5 and 5 mm
32 in / 80 cm circulars US sizes 7 and 8 / 4.5 and 5 mm for collar
Cable needle

Gauge   17 sts × 24 rows in stockinette on needles US 8 / 5 mm = 4 × 4 in / 10 × 10 cm
1 repeat in length = 32 rows = 5¼ in / 13 cm
Adjust needle sizes to obtain correct gauge if necessary.

Edge stitches This garment is worked without any special edge stitches. The outermost st at each side is used for seaming.

Note This sweater can be worn by either a man or woman; only the sleeves are different.

Chart Braided Hearts, p. 168.

Double Broken Rib (multiple of 4+2 sts)
Row 1 (RS): Knit
Row 2: Purl
Row 3: *K2, p2; repeat from * and end with k2
Row 4: *P2, k2; repeat from * and end with p2
Repeat these 4 rows.

Back
With larger needles, cast on 86 (94, 102, 110, 118, 126) sts. Work in k2, p2 ribbing for 3½ in / 9 cm, beginning on WS with p2, k2. Change to Double Broken Rib pattern. When piece measures 16½ in / 42 cm (ending with pattern Row 4), shape armholes by first binding off 2 sts at each side. Next, decrease 1 st on every other row 5 times = 72 (80, 88, 96, 104, 112) sts remain. When armhole measures 9½ (9¾, 10¼, 10¾, 11, 11½) in / 24 (25, 26, 27, 28, 29) cm (after Row 4 of pattern), place the center 30 (30, 30, 34, 34, 34) sts on a holder and bind off 21 (25, 29, 31, 35, 39) sts using a separate thread for each shoulder.

Front
Work as for back until front measures 13 (13½, 13¾, 13¾, 14¼, 14½) in / 33 (34, 35, 35, 36, 37) cm (after Row 2 of pattern). Place marker at each side of the center 18 sts—there should be 2 knit ribs on each side of these sts. Continue in pattern except for the 18 sts between markers; work

these sts as: purl 1 row, knit 2 rows, purl 1 row and then continue with the 16-st Braided Hearts motif bordered by 1 st reverse stockinette at each side of motif. After completing charted rows, knit 1 row, purl 2 rows, knit 1 row over the 18 center sts and then bind off the center 18 sts. Work each side separately.

Left side: Cast on an edge st at neck edge and decrease as follows: Work until 4 sts remain at neck edge, k2tog, k2. This allows the knit rib inside the edge st to follow the neckline. Decrease the same way on every 6th row 7 (7, 7, 9, 9, 9) times total. When armhole measures 9½ (9¾, 10¼, 10¾, 11, 11½) in / 24 (25, 26, 27, 28, 29) cm (after Row 4 of pattern), bind off 21 (25, 29, 31, 35, 39) sts for shoulder.

Right side: Work as for left side, reversing shaping and decreasing at neck edge as follows: K2, ssk, work to end of row as set.

Sleeves

With larger needles, cast on 42 (42, 42, 46, 46, 46) sts. Work in k2, p2 ribbing for 3½ in / 9 cm, beginning on WS with p2, k2. Change to Double Broken Rib pattern. *At the same time,* begin shaping sleeve by increasing 1 st at each side on every 4th row 22 (23, 25, 24, 26, 27) times = 86 (88, 92, 94, 98, 100) sts. Work all new sts into pattern. When sleeve is 18¼ in / 46 cm long for women and 20½ in / 52 cm for men (ending with pattern Row 4), shape sleeve cap by first binding off 2 sts at each side (this should be over a knit rib). Next, decrease 1 st at each side on every other row 5 times and then bind off remaining 72 (74, 78, 80, 84, 86) sts.

Finishing

Block pieces. Undo bound-off sts and join shoulders with three-needle bind-off.

Collar: With smaller size circular, pick up and knit 42 (44, 46, 46, 48, 50) sts along left front edge, 30 (30, 30, 34, 34, 34) sts along back neck, and 42 (44, 46, 46, 48, 50) sts along right front = 114 (118, 122, 126, 130, 134) sts.

Place a marker at each shoulder. K 1 row and increase 6 sts evenly spaced between markers = 120 (124, 128, 132, 136, 140) sts total.

Purl 2 rows, knit 2 rows, purl 1 row. Change to larger circular and work in k2, p2 ribbing beginning and ending row with k3 on RS of garment).

Now shape the collar with short rows: Work past one shoul-

der seam and over to the other seam; turn after the first purl rib. Work back to the first shoulder and turn after the first purl rib. Now work each row with 4 more sts than the previous row until you are once again working across all sts on the row (the final 2 short rows will end with 3 or 5 sts). Continue in ribbing for about 4¾ in / 12 cm so that it matches the bound-off sts at the front. Bind off loosely in ribbing (you may want to use a larger size needle). Overlap the collar and seam the short ends of the collar to the bound-off sts at front. Sew sleeve and side seams. Attach sleeves.

UNN child's sizes

Sizes   2 (4, 6, 8, 10, 12) years

Finished measurements

Chest   26¾ (28¼, 30, 31½, 33, 35½) in
            68 (72, 76, 80, 84, 90) cm

Length   14¼ (15¾, 17¼, 19, 20½, 22¾) in
            36 (40, 44, 48, 52, 58) cm

Materials

Yarn   Silky Wool (p. 14)

Yarn amounts 150 (200, 200, 250, 250, 300) g

Needles

            US sizes 4 and 6 / 3.5 and 4 mm
            32 or 24 in / 80 or 60 cm circular US sizes
            4 and 6 / 3.5 and 4 mm for collar
            Cable needle

Gauge   22 sts × 30 rows in stockinette on larger
            needles = 4 × 4 in / 10 × 10 cm

Adjust needle sizes to obtain correct gauge if necessary.

Edge stitches This garment is worked without any special edge stitches. The outermost st at each side is used for seaming.

Chart Braided Hearts, p. 168.

Double Broken Rib (multiple of 4+2 sts)

Row 1 (RS): Knit

Row 2: Purl

Row 3: *K2, p2; repeat from * and end with k2

Row 4: *P2, k2; repeat from * and end with p2

Repeat these 4 rows.

Back

With larger needles, cast on 78 (82, 86, 90, 94, 102) sts. Work in k2, p2 ribbing for 2 (2, 2, 2½, 2½, 2½) in / 5 (5, 5, 6, 6, 6) cm, beginning on WS with p2, k2. Change to Double Broken Rib pattern. When piece measures 8¾ (9¾, 10¾, 11¾, 12½, 14½) in / 22 (25, 27, 30, 32, 37) cm (ending with pattern Row 4), shape armholes by first binding off 1 st at each side. Next, decrease 1 st on every other row 2 times = 72 (76, 80, 84, 88, 96) sts remain. When work measures 14¼ (15¾, 17, 19, 20½, 22¾) in / 36 (40) 43 (48) 52 (58) cm (after Row 4 of pattern), place the center 26 (26, 30, 30, 34, 34) sts on a holder and, using a separate strand for each shoulder, bind off 23 (25, 25, 27, 27, 31) sts.

Front

Work as for back until front measures 4¾ (6, 6¾, 8¼, 9½, 12¼) in / 12 (15, 17, 21, 24, 31) cm (after Row 2 of pattern). Place marker at each side of the center 18 sts—there should be 2 knit ribs on each side of these sts. Continue in pattern except for the 18 sts between markers; work these sts as: purl 1 row, knit 2 rows, purl 1 row and then continue with the 16-st Braided Hearts motif bordered by 1 st reverse stockinette at each side of motif. After completing charted rows, knit 1 row, purl 2 rows, knit 1 row over the 18 center sts and then bind off the center 18 sts. Work each side separately.

Left side: Cast on an edge st at neck edge and decrease as follows: Work until 4 sts remain at neck edge, k2tog, k2. This allows the knit rib inside the edge st to follow the neckline. Decrease the same way on every 6th (6th, 8th, 8th, 8th, 8th) row 4 (4, 6, 6, 8, 8) more times. When piece measures 14¼ (15¾, 17, 19, 20½, 22¾) in / 36 (40, 43, 48, 52, 58) cm (after Row 4 of pattern), bind off remaining 23 (25, 25, 27, 27, 31) sts for shoulder.

Right side: Work as for left side, reversing shaping and decreasing at neck edge as follows: K2, ssk, work to end of row as set.

Sleeves

With larger needles, cast on 34 (34, 38, 38, 42, 42) sts. Work in k2, p2 ribbing for 2 (2, 2, 2½, 2½, 2½ in / 5 (5) 5 (6) 6 (6) cm, beginning on WS with p2, k2. Change to Double Broken Rib pattern. *At the same time*, begin shaping sleeve by increasing 1 st at each side on every 4th row 14 (14, 14, 16, 18, 20) times and then on every other row 0 (2, 4, 4, 4, 4) times = 62 (66, 74, 78, 86, 90) sts. Work all new sts into pattern. When sleeve is 9¾ (11½, 13, 14¼, 15¼, 16½) in / 25 (29, 33, 36, 39, 42) cm long (ending with pattern Row 4), shape sleeve cap by first binding off 1 st at each side. Next, decrease 1 st at each side on every other row 2 times and then bind off the remaining sts.

Finishing

Block pieces. Undo bound-off sts and join shoulders with three-needle bind-off.

Collar: With smaller size circular, pick up and knit 34 (38, 42, 44, 48, 52) sts along left front edge, 26 (26, 30, 30, 34, 34) sts along back neck, and 34 (38, 42, 44, 48, 52) sts along right front edge = 94 (102, 114, 118, 130, 138) sts. Place a marker at each shoulder. K 1 row and increase 6 sts evenly spaced between markers = 100 (108, 120, 124, 136, 144) sts total.

Purl 2 rows, knit 2 rows, purl 1 row. Change to larger circular and work in k2, p2 ribbing beginning and ending with k3 at each side on RS of garment.

Now shape the collar with short rows: Work past one shoulder seam and over to the other seam; turn after the first purl rib. Work back to the first shoulder and turn after the first purl rib. Now work each row with 4 more sts than the previous row until you are once again working across all sts on the row (the final 2 short rows will end with 3 or 5 sts). Continue in ribbing for about 3¼ in / 8 cm so that it matches the bound-off sts at the front. Bind off loosely in ribbing (you may want to use a larger size needle). Overlap the collar and seam the short ends of the collar to the bound-off sts at front. Sew sleeve and side seams. Attach sleeves.

The depicted mount from Valsgärde, Sweden, shows how easily braided patterns can grow and develop: Follow the progression (bottom to top) from the Skabersjö motif into two mirrored Overhand Knots, back to the Skabersjö motif and finally turning into an intriguing adaptation of a Six Band Braid. I can't really think of a cooler way to sum up what I find so fascinating about the ornamental universe presented in this book.

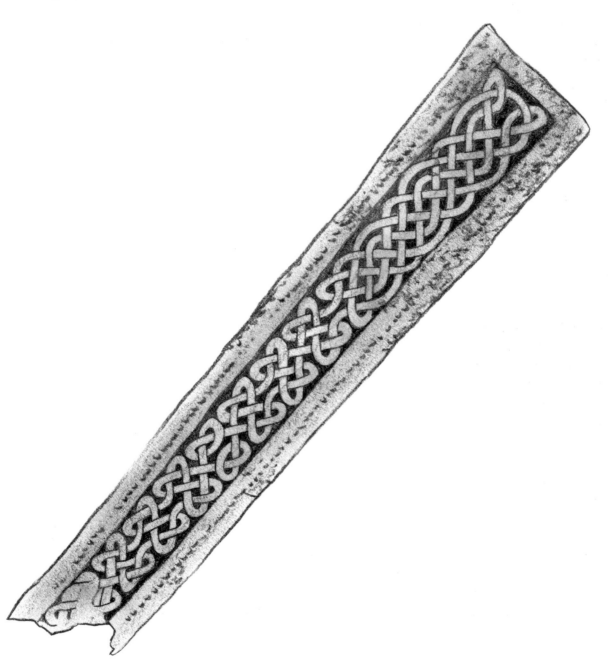

The Grammar of Viking Cables

Viking cable patterns feature plain bands, consisting of two stockinette stitches, moving across a reverse stockinette stitch background. It is possible to use other background patterns, such as moss stitch or double moss stitch, but here I will use reverse stockinette which is stockinette using the reverse side as the public side.

The cable pattern bands can move across the background, vertically and diagonally but *not* horizontally. As opposed to the bands in traditional cable patterns, which always move upwards, the bands of a Viking cable pattern can change direction and move downwards and upwards again and tie themselves into knots. This opens up a whole world of new possibilities.

These bands can start at the beginning or at almost any point in the knitting. This is made possible by increasing and decreasing systematically inside the knitting. These increases and decreases combine several functions; they create and eliminate the bands at strategic points, giving the cable pattern its shape, and they form the turning points of the bands. And, as if that wasn't enough, they compensate for the pulling together of the fabric that is caused by the cable crossings. This technique, using lifted increases, provides a systematic and relatively easy method for knitting cabled motifs without deforming the background and without affecting the gauge.

In most Viking cable patterns you will find that when four stockinette stitches meet they will cross in the same direction across the entire row. Several rows later, when four stockinette stitches meet again, they will cross in the opposite direction. This leads to the effect that, if you follow any given band in the pattern, it will always weave over and under and over and under the other bands in a systematic way. This makes the patterns easy to learn and to remember, and therefore easy to knit (easy at their skill level, that is).

Another effect is that all patterns have two variants depending on the direction of the plain crossings on the same row in the pattern. The character of the pattern will remain the same, though (actually it can be difficult to even notice the difference). So, if you happen to start off crossing your plain cable crossings in the wrong direction, just continue doing that in all the following plain crossings so that you retain the weaving over and under of the bands.

The fact that the pattern is created almost solely on the right side, where you can see what is happening, means that you can "rest" on the wrong side rows where you always knit the knits and purl the purls. The only exception is the last decrease which is made on the wrong side. But you are always tipped off about that by the preceding decrease row. Just remember; decrease on the right side followed by decrease on the wrong side, and then you're done. This means that you really don't have to read the chart for the wrong side rows.

The basic elements of Viking cable patterns

The basic structure of the patterns, or the flow of the knitting if you will, goes like this:

You start by placing your increase group followed by a centered or directional beginning.

Next you will be making right-slanting plain crossings and working plain stockinette on 2-stitch bands followed by a row where the bands will move across the background. On the following row you'll be making left-slanting plain crossings and working plain stockinette on 2-stitch bands followed by another row of bands moving across the background. At the sides, when there are only 2 plain stitches, they should be worked in stockinette.

This moving across the background and left and right crossings will go on for as long as the pattern requires, but at some point you will want it to end.

You then move into your centered or directional ending which is finished with the decrease group.

Increases and decreases

The group of increases is identical in all Viking cable patterns. The increases are made in pairs, each increase the mirror image of the other, on two consecutive right side rows. This is only possible using lifted increases. The increases are creating the stitches that will become the bands for the cable pattern. This means that the increased stitches must always be knitted on the right side (and purled on the wrong side). Remember that the increase symbol represents the increased stitch, *not the foundation stitch* into which it is made. The left lifted increase is made into the preceding stitch and will be positioned to the left of that stitch. The right lifted increase is made into the following stitch and will be positioned to the right of it. See pp. 187–188.

The group of decreases is identical in all Viking cable patterns. The decreases are also mirror image pairs, but they are made on two consecutive rows. And they are made the exact same way on both sides, an ssk followed by a k2tog, *but they produce different results!* The first decrease, made on the right side, reduces each band to one stockinette stitch. The second decrease, identical but made on the wrong side, eliminates the final stockinette stitches, leaving only the reverse stockinette background stitches on the right side and a smooth unbroken stockinette fabric on the wrong side.

The group of increases The group of decreases

Beginnings and endings

Once you have placed your increases and created your two bands, there are only three things that can happen:

Centered Beginning: The two bands move away from each other.

Directional Beginning: One band moves away from the other which continues straight up. The band can move to the right or to the left.

In the same manner, there are only three options for endings:

Centered Ending: Both bands moving together and meeting.

Directional Ending: One band moving straight up while the other moves in from the side until they meet. As for the directional beginning, the band can move in from either right or left.

Cable crossings

There are only six ways of crossing your cables:

Two knits crossed over two knits to the left or to the right
Two knits crossed over two purls to the left or to the right
Two knits crossed over one purl to the left or to the right

Crossing two stitches over two creates an almost 45 degree slant, whereas two stitches crossed over one will give you a steeper slant.

Directional Ending Left   *Centered Ending*   *Directional Ending Right*

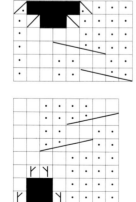   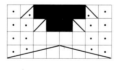   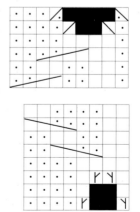

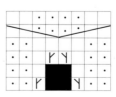

Directional Beginning Left   *Centered Beginning*   *Directional Beginning Right*

Creating your own patterns

When you create your own patterns, versions or variations, it is usually best to start analyzing and charting the central part of the pattern first (the rows with the maximum number of stitches) and position the groups of increases and decreases later and then, at the end, position the black squares. Their function is just to ensure that the stitches are aligned vertically in the same manner as the stitches in the knitting.

So, as you have seen, the increases provide the stitches for the bands that make up the pattern. I recommend that you always make sure that you have at least four rows of reverse stockinette below the first increase. The increases are made in the row below and will "eat" that row, leaving only three of the four rows visible. Two rows of reverse stockinette after the last decrease will provide the same amount of fabric visually, as the last decrease produces purls, leaving you with three rows of reverse stockinette above the pattern.

The construction of the patterns, with a row of movement across background alternating with a row of plain crossings, leads to most patterns having a row count divisible by four.

In panels, the cable pattern is connected to vertical bands. The number of purl stitches for the background and the number of stitches for the vertical bands will not change as the work progresses, so the stitches for the vertical bands must be included when you cast on. This also means that when you start knitting from the chart, only the purls (square with a dot) and stockinette stitches of vertical bands (empty square) exist. The cable knots will be created with increases and decreases as you go and increased stitches will usually be eliminated before you reach the end.

Be sure to count stitches only on rows without increased stitches, or make sure you don't count the increased stitches. Once in a while though, you will have to bind off or place stitches on a holder when you are in a pattern section with increased stitches. You will have to account for these extra stitches at an appropriate place in your garment. This most often happens at the back neck resulting in more stitches at the back neck than at the front neck.

Abbreviations

cm	centimeter(s)
cn	cable needle
dpn	double-pointed needles
in	inch(es)
k	knit
k2tog	knit 2 sts together
k3tog	knit 3 sts together
LC	left cable
LLI	left lifted increase
M1	make 1: lift the strand between 2 sts and knit into back loop
M1p	make 1 purl: lift the strand between 2 sts and purl into back loop
mm	millimeter(s)
p	purl
p2tog	purl 2 sts together
RC	right cable
RLI	right lifted increase
RS	right side
ssk	slip, slip, knit (knit the 2 slipped sts together through back loops)
st(s)	stitch(es)
tog	together
WS	wrong side

Creating Cable Patterns

There are numerous ways of perceiving interlace patterns in regard to their construction. You can look at how knots are tied, or concentrate on the mathematical aspect. On the Internet, there's actually a knot atlas aspiring to become a complete center of information on knot theory, a mathematical discipline. The decorative aspect is the main feature from an artistic perspective. The inspiration may derive from practical use of knots, but also from basket weaving and fabric weaving, both among the most ancient crafts.

The Irish interlace patterns have been subject to extensive studies since they became an important aspect of Celtic identity among the peoples, Irish, Scottish and Welsh, who had been living under the shadow of the British Empire and the English culture.

In the 1930's, J. Romilly Allen created a typology of Celtic knots. He divided them into eight types, three of which are derived from the three-cord plait and the rest from the four-cord plait (his terminology).

It is an interesting effort and this approach can be fruitful although I don't consider his analysis deep enough. For example, the loops of knots 4, 5 and 7 are identical, just placed in different manners.

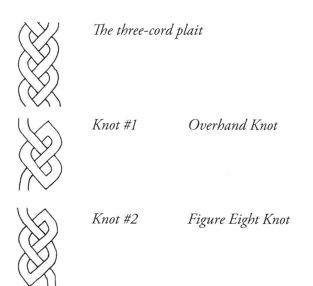

The three-cord plait

Knot #1   *Overhand Knot*

Knot #2   *Figure Eight Knot*

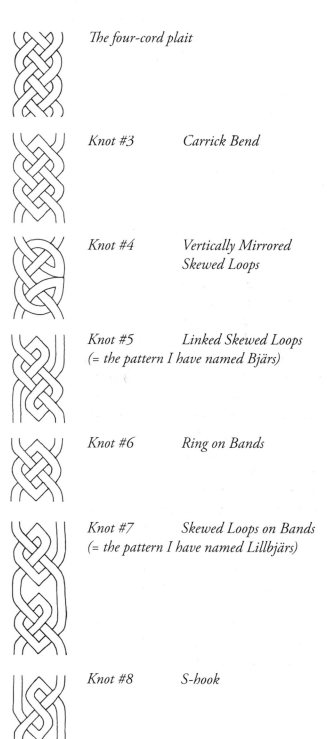

The four-cord plait

Knot #3   *Carrick Bend*

Knot #4   *Vertically Mirrored Skewed Loops*

Knot #5   *Linked Skewed Loops (= the pattern I have named Bjärs)*

Knot #6   *Ring on Bands*

Knot #7   *Skewed Loops on Bands (= the pattern I have named Lillbjärs)*

Knot #8   *S-hook*

I will here try to take Allen's analysis farther as well as adding a knitter's perspective.

The Basic Elements

There are several perspectives that can be applied when creating patterns, i.e. the same pattern can be viewed in different ways. Here are some, hopefully fruitful, pointers.

Bands

The patterns consist of stockinette bands traveling across a background. They can move vertically and diagonally and cross each other in different directions.

Bands placed parallel to each other can be braided; two can be twisted, three, four and six can be interlaced in different ways. Of course any numbers of bands can be used, but in this book I concentrate on the aforementioned.

The Two Band Twist is of course not strictly speaking a braid, but is included for its close ties (pardon the pun) to the other patterns and for its decorative possibilities. The bands of the Three, Four and Six Band Braids can be manipulated endlessly by switching between left and right crossings and their placement horizontally and vertically.

The bands, at least when you have an even number, can be joined at the ends, either symmetrically or asymmetrically.

Ring

Two bands joined at both ends will create a ring motif. In mathematical knot theory this is an unknot. The ring is in principle round but in knitting it will be rather diamond shaped. It can be widened, elongated or extended diagonally to create a rhomboid. The possibilities abound.

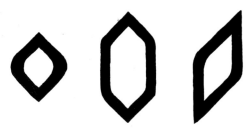

Ring, Elongated Ring and Rhomboid

The ring in any of its incarnations can be manipulated by twisting in one or several places. Each twist creates a crossing either to the left or to the right. The distance between crossings can be varied to create different sizes and shapes

of the parts in between. All of the following patterns are unknots; a twist in the middle will create a *Figure Eight*, two twists evenly spaced becomes a *Two Band Twist*, a twist at the top and one at the bottom will create a *Looped Ring*, a twist in each corner will create a *Fourknot*.

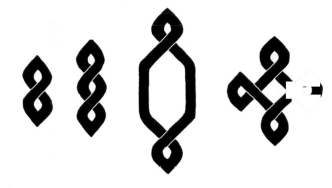

Loops

Crossing the ends of a band will create a loop. Loops can have four orientations; up, down, right and left.

Four loop orientations

The loops can be connected and manipulated in different manners; connecting two loops at the crossing, creating a *Figure Eight* or connecting the legs for a *Two Band Twist*. Connecting the legs of all four orientations makes a *Fourknot*.

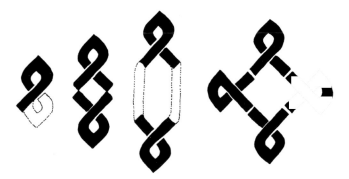

Combinations

So here we have a number of elements, Band, Ring, Loop, in different versions that can be combined in different manners. A ring can be linked with a ring or linked into a loop. A band can be woven into a ring or through a loop.

Loops can be connected to and braided together with bands or with a ring. The possibilities are endless.

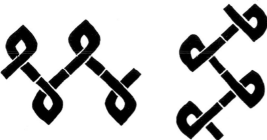

Knots

One of the most natural things to do with a band is to make an *Overhand Knot*. This means that you make a loop and pull one end of the band through the loop. If you don't tighten the knot it will look like a pretzel and the band will enter and exit the loop on the same side. Pull the band through the loop one more time and you'll get a *Figure Eight Knot*. Now the band will enter on one side and exit on the opposite side. Both these knots are very decorative.

Continue pulling the band through the loop any number of times (embroiderers will recognize the French Knot). Every other time the band will exit on the same or on opposite sides. If you continue, the knot will turn into a *Three Band Braid*.

Principles of panel construction

Panels are created when pattern elements are repeated vertically and can be constructed in many ways. The shape of the pattern element will affect the construction of the panel. The following are useful principles for panel construction. In all cases, remember to adjust all stockinette crossings to maintain the over-under principle.

One-band panels

This is the obvious choice for pattern elements where the bands enter and exit on the same side, like the Overhand Knot. This means that the knot part of the pattern extends from one vertical band.

By working with mirror images of the pattern you can connect them so that the knots extend from the band in opposite directions or even exaggerate this effect by making the band move in a zigzag with knots at the turning points.

These bands with their knots can then be combined in different ways. An easy way to create a pretty panel is to place a vertical band without knots on the "open" side of the pattern, so that the knots are visually framed on both sides. Vertical bands can be placed back to back for a symmetrical panel or placed zipper wise for a framed asymmetrical panel e.g. *Wing Loop Twisted & Staggered*. Two zigzag panels can be interlaced and the meeting point can be the center point of another knot detail, etc.

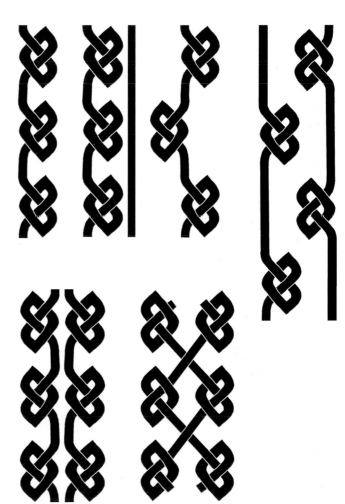

Even patterns with opposing entry and exit can be turned into one-band patterns by connecting them with a diagonal or by mirroring every other repeat.

Opposing entry and exit is ideal for creating diagonal patterns. Simply connecting the exiting band of one repeat to the entering band of the next will make the pattern move diagonally across the background.

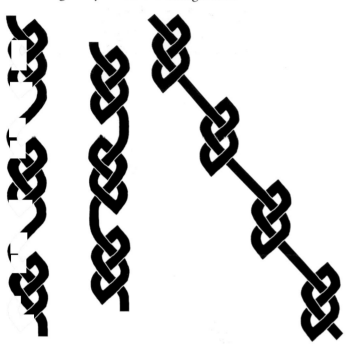

Two-band panels

For patterns with opposing entry and exit, the two-band principle is a good solution. The S-hook is a good example. The S-hook is basically a diagonal with opposing hooks at each end. Here a second band is woven through the S and creates an opposing diagonal. In the next repeat the bands change function; the S-hook becomes a plain diagonal and the diagonal becomes an S-hook.

This is the principle of all two-band patterns. The main issue is finding a way to weave the diagonal through the knot without changing its character. Many motifs can be braided into two crossing bands.

Three-band panels

In three-band panels the patterns rotate in three steps. This is suitable for patterns with one band entering and exiting on the same side and one entering and exiting on opposing sides. These patterns have three functions that rotate; the knot, the diagonal and a third band that moves more or less vertically.

Horizontal borders

Many pattern elements can be arranged so that they create horizontal borders. An illustrative example is the loop where two vertically mirrored loops can be connected to create a horizontal loop border, *Loop Horizontal Zigzag*. In the *Horizontal S-hook Border* the S-hooks are connected every other time at the top and at the bottom.

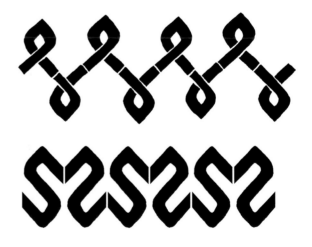

All-over patterns

Some patterns can be connected both vertically and horizontally to create all-over patterns. Another way is to make a lattice of diagonal bands and weave in knot motifs where the bands cross.

Do it yourself

Now that you have read the theoretical aspects of how to manipulate and vary patterns, my advice to you is knit and don't think too much—follow your intuition.

Adding Color

It is entirely possible to knit these patterns with the cabling in a contrasting color using a combination of Intarsia and stranding.

For a motif like the Little Knot & Ring used here I've stranded both the main color and the pattern color and just turned the pattern color, without twisting the yarn, at the end of the motif. For patterns with long vertical stretches, you'll want to use Intarsia technique, using a separate ball of yarn for each area of color, twisting the yarns (only once around) at the color change to avoid holes. Each color will make a U-turn at the meeting point.

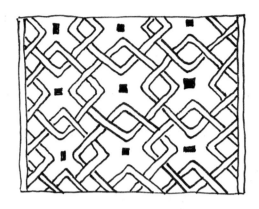

Technical Information

Techniques

These are my preferred techniques for knitting and finishing. My patterns are written for using them since I find that working in this manner makes the finishing easier and gives a more beautiful result. Feel free to use whichever techniques you prefer.

Casting on

Long-tail or continental cast-on

I normally use the long-tail or continental cast-on. It has one side which looks more refined than the other. The first row is worked on the wrong side so that the nicer-looking edge will show on the right side. For this reason, all edgings have an odd number of rows. Casting on over two needles held together will make the cast-on row more elastic.

Edge stitches

The outermost stitch at each side is an edge st. Edge sts are included in the stitch counts and are always knitted unless otherwise specified. A size marker in a chart points to a stitch which should be worked as an edge st.

Decreases

I often decrease within the edge stitches by working k2tog at the beginning of a row and ssk at the end of a row unless otherwise specified. It is easier to decrease on the smooth side of the work regardless of whether it is the right or wrong side.

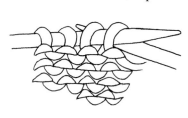

ssk: one at a time, slip 2 sts as if to knit. Knit them together through back loops. Slipping the stitches will turn them so that, when you knit them together through the back loops, they will not be twisted (a mirror image of k2tog).

When you shape a piece by binding off stitches, be sure to slip the first stitch to avoid a stairstep along the edge.

Increases

I usually increase using a right lifted increase (RLI) at the beginning of a row and a left lifted increase (LLI) at the end (see p. 188).

Stitches on hold

When instructions say place stitches on a holder, I recommend binding off using waste yarn as it makes blocking easier. When picking up the stitches again, just unravel the bound-off edge.

Short rows

Short rows are used to shape the knitting. Sometimes I use them for edgings and collars but I nearly always use them to shape shoulders. There will be a two-row difference in height at each turning point. Slipping the first st after turning and pulling the yarn tightly will be enough to avoid a gap in most cases. If you want to minimize the gap at the turning point, you should use either the wrap & turn method or the yarnover method, both of which can be found in books about knitting techniques, in knitting magazines or you can use your favorite Internet search engine to find "short rows."

Whichever method you prefer, you will end up with live sts that you can place on a holder or bind off temporarily. The temporary bind-off will leave enough yarn to knit the shoulders together using the three-needle bind-off.

Three-needle bind-off for knitting shoulders together

Place pieces with right sides facing each other and needles pointing in the same direction. K2tog (1 st from each needle), repeat this and pass the first stitch over the second. Continue in this manner, knitting one st from each needle and binding off as usual.

Blocking

Blocking pieces before finishing will even out the knitting and make the finishing easier.

I have a blocking board, a soft fiber board covered with a block patterned fabric (to make pinning easier), but a soft carpet and/or some towels will do.

Start by pinning the back onto the board, laying it out in the correct shape according to the measurements. Then spray the piece with water using an atomizer. To ensure that the front or fronts will have the same shape as the back, pin it, or them, on top of the back, and spray again. Do the same with the two sleeves, pinning one on top of the other, spraying the first and then the second sleeve. You don't have to soak the pieces, just dampen them. That done, all you have to do is wait for them to dry.

 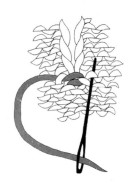

Seams

Most seams will look their best if grafted together with mattress stitch from the right side, although backstitching inside the edge stitch will do for most side and sleeve seams. Set-in sleeves need the extra stability of backstitching.

It is almost impossible to make seams in reverse stockinette really beautiful. Therefore, for many of the designs, to achieve a neater result and make seaming easier, I have added a stockinette rib along the edges that are to be seamed. Work k2 at the beginning and end of all right side rows and purl the sts inside the edge st on all wrong side rows. This will form a knit rib when the side seams and sleeves are joined. Increase inside these 2 sts. Such ribs can be added on any design that has reverse stockinette sections at the sides.

I-cord

With 2 double pointed needles, cast on 3 (4) sts: k3 (4), * do not turn work; instead, slide sts to front of left needle and knit them. Repeat from * throughout. When I-cord reaches desired length, cut yarn and pull tail through sts.

Or, pick up sts along the edge and knit the I-cord onto the piece.

Reading Charts

A chart is like a map of a pattern, showing how the pattern looks on the right side.

Each square in the chart equals a stitch of knitting. A horizontal row of squares corresponds to a row of knitting and a vertical row of squares represents stitches aligned above each other in the knitting. The right side rows are odd-numbered and are read from right to left; wrong side rows are read from left to right, although generally you won't need to read the wrong side rows (this is explained in more detail on p. 176).

In Viking cable patterns, the stitch count varies between sections of the pattern. The charts are drawn so that the largest number of stitches can be shown. On rows with fewer stitches, black squares are inserted so that stitches which are worked directly above each other can be shown that way in the chart. These black squares have no meaning for the knitting! When you come to a black square in the chart, skip it and go to the next square that is not black and work it as indicated. Be sure to count stitches only on rows without increased stitches.

The fact that the chart shows the pattern as seen from the right side means that the stitches need to be worked differently depending on whether the symbol is placed on a right side row or a wrong side row. The symbols are explained in the list on p. 187 and the techniques are shown in detail on p. 188.

An empty square represents stockinette stitch and is knitted on the right side and purled on the wrong side. Reverse stockinette is represented by the dot and worked the opposite way, purled on the right and knitted on the wrong side. Apart from these two symbols, only decrease symbols appear on both right and wrong side rows and, although different symbols are used in the chart, the pairs of decreases are worked *exactly the same way on both sides but with different results*. The slant of the decrease symbols shows the slant of the actual decrease.

The increase symbol represents *the increased stitch*, not the foundation stitch into which it is made. The left lifted increase is made into the preceding stitch and will be positioned to the left of that stitch. The right lifted increase is made into the following stitch and will be positioned to the right of it. See p. 188.

The cable crossings are represented by diagonal lines across several squares, the slant showing the slant of the crossing. The number of squares will show how many stitches are involved. If there are dots in any of the squares, the crossing will be knit over purl; otherwise, it will be knit over knit (the knit stitches are always in front of the purls).

For garments, a group of stitches may need to be repeated. Such a group of stitches is called a "repeat" and will be marked on the chart between bold lines. Always start knitting from the beginning of the chart if nothing else is indicated. Work to the first repeat line, then work the repeat the required number of times and end with the part of the chart that remains after the second repeat line. Most of my designs are symmetrical, so, you will end the row as it began.

Some charts will also have bold horizontal lines. These are sections of the pattern that may be repeated between the knots. This will be dealt with in the pattern text.

My charts are usually drawn with 2 background stitches at each side and 2 rows of plain reverse stockinette before the first increase and after the last decrease.

Chart Symbols

☐ knit on Right Side, purl on Wrong Side

• purl on Right Side, knit on Wrong Side

+ knit on Right Side, knit on Wrong Side

╱ k2 together on Right Side

╲ ssk on Right Side

╲ k2 together on Wrong Side

╱ ssk on Wrong Side

Υ right lifted increase

Υ left lifted increase

■ no stitch

2/1 Right Purl Cable: slip 1 st to cn, hold to back, k2; p1 from cn

2/1 Left Purl Cable: slip 2 sts to cn, hold to front, p1; k2 from cn;

2/2 Right Cable: slip 2 st to cn, hold to back, k2; k2 from cn

2/2 Left Cable: slip 2 sts to cn, hold to front, k2; k2 from cn

2/2 Right Purl Cable: slip 2 st to cn, hold to back, k2; p2 from cn

2/2 Left Purl Cable: slip 2 sts to cn, hold to front, p2; k2 from cn

The Lifted Increases used in Viking Knits Designs

The drawings below are placed the same way that the increases are placed in the actual knitting.

The increases are all made on the Right Side, with the reverse stockinette facing. The increased stitches will all be knit stitches, they will create the bands of the pattern, and must be purled on the wrong side rows.

The first two increases are an LLI followed by an RLI in a purl st. The second pair of increases are made *between* the first two increases; first an LLI, then an RLI in a knit st.

4 Right Lifted Increase in a knit stitch: Go in from the back of the knitting, into the purl st just below the first stitch on the left needle. Insert the point of your right needle into the center of that stitch and pull back in such a way that you catch only the top of it. Place it on the left needle and *knit* into the front or back so it does not get twisted.

3 Left Lifted Increase in a knit stitch: Go in from the back of the knitting, into the purl st 2 steps down from the last stitch on the right needle. Insert the point of your left needle into the center of that stitch and pull back in such a way that you catch only the top of it. Place it on the left needle and *knit* into the front or back so it does not get twisted.

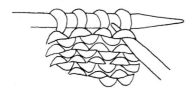

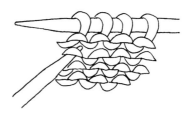

2 Right Lifted Increase in a purl stitch: Lift the purl st just below the first stitch on the left needle (which has not been purled yet) and *knit* it.
You may have to place it on the right needle in order to be able knit it.

1 Left Lifted Increase in a purl stitch: Lift the purl st 2 steps down from the last stitch on the right needle (which has already been purled) and *knit* it.

The Patterns

Bjärs Motif Left & Right	74
Bjärs Pointed Motif Left	74
Bjärs Pointed Motif Right	75
Braided Figure Eights	62
Braided Hearts	168
Braided Loops	18
Braided Wing Loops	24
Chain Narrow	48
Chain Wide	49
Cross on Bands	155
Dalby Left & Right	118
Dalby Up & Down	119
Downwards Pointing Loop	16
Elongated Ring	47
Eternal Knot	162
Eternal Knot Pointed	163
Figure Eight & Ring	60
Figure Eight on Band Left & Right	55
Figure Eight Variations	54
Figure Eights on Crossed Bands	56
Four Band Braid	154
Fourknot Cutoff Down	94
Fourknot Cutoff Up	94
Hausa Knot	160
Large Figure Eight	53
Large Ring	44
Lillbjärs Mirrored Panel	38
Lillbjärs Staggered	37
Little Knot & Fourknot	91
Little Knot & Ring	88
Little Knot & Ring on Cable	88
Little Knot Extended	84
Little Knot More Extended	84

Little Knot More Stretched	85
Little Knot Stretched	85
Looped Ring	63
Looped Ring Chain & Chain	67
Looped Ring Chain Narrow	66
Looped Ring Chain Wide	66
Looped Ring on Bands	63
Looped Ring on Cross	63
Looped Ring on Figure Eight	65
Multiple Overhand Knot Left & Right	115
Overhand Knot on Bands	116
Overhand Knot Motif	116
Ring on Cross	45
Ring on Double Bands	46
Rings on Bands	46
S-hook	127
S-hook Horizontal Border	142
S-hook Horizontal Interlaced Border	143
S-hook Horizontal Motif Up & Down	144
S-hook Interlaced Meander Narrow	138
S-hook Interlaced Meander Wide	138
S-hook Labyrinth Left	130
S-hook Labyrinth Right	131
S-hook Motif Left & Right	135
S-hook Pointed	127
Six Band Braid	158
Skabersjö on Bands	163
Three Band Braid	153
Threeknot Base Upwards & Downwards	108
Threeknot Downwards	99
Threeknot Elongated	103
Threeknot Upwards	99
Trondheim Left	124

Continued on next page

Trondheim Right 125
Twisted Wing Loop Down Left 27
Twisted Wing Loop Down on Cable 28
Twisted Wing Loop Down Right 27
Twisted Wing Loop Up Left 27
Twisted Wing Loop Up on Cable 28
Twisted Wing Loop Up Right 26
Two Band Twist 150

Upwards Pointing Loop 16

Vendel Loop Down Left & Right 33
Vendel Loop Up Left & Right 32
Vertical Zigzag Loops 22

Wing Loop Left & Right 20
Wing Loops on Bands 21
Wing Loops on Cable 20
Wing Loops Motif 21
Wing Loops Twisted & Staggered 25

Z-Hook 127
Z-Hook Pointed 127

Acknowledgements

We would like to thank the following museums for being so generous regarding photography permissions:

Croatia
Muzej Lapidarium, Novigrad,

Italy
Musei Civici di Como
Museo Archeologico Nazionale di Aquileia
Museo Nazionale Paleocristiano, Aquileia
Museo Archeologico Nazionale di Cividale del Friuli
Santa Giulia Museo, Brescia

Malta
Domvs Romana, Rabat

Sweden
The Historical Museum, Stockholm
Gotlands Fornsal, Visby

We also want to thank the following for allowing us to use their premises as background for some of our photography:

Gunnes gård, Upplands Väsby, a reconstructed Viking farm near Stockholm. Open to the public during the summer months.

Frösåkers brygga, Västerås, a reconstructed Viking village and harbor an hour's drive from Stockholm. Open to the public during the summer months.

Viking age sword handle found in Grötlingbo, Gotland, Sweden

My Heartfelt Thanks

Just as for *Viking Patterns for Knitting,* the work on this book has progressed at its own pace for more than a decade. Many people have contributed in different ways in making it possible.

First and foremost and with great appreciation, I thank my wonderful knitters: Eva Hallberg, Gerd Härnvall, Gullevi Ljungström, Helena Norén, Lotta Persson, Pia Persson and Bertil Rejnevi, whose skill and dedication is a prerequisite for the realization of my ideas. Thank you, you are all wonderful! I want to direct a particular thank you to my dear friend, Helena Norén, who has worked with me closely since the early 80's. Your professionalism, speed, and willingness to take on impossible jobs have saved my bacon many a time.

I also want to honor three knitters who are not among us any longer, but who were very involved in the Viking Project at different stages: Irma Hansen, Brita Löwenadler and Solveig Näslund. I hope you are happy in knitting heaven!

Much appreciation for my dear friends: Carol Rhoades for her dedication and skill in translation and technical editing and patience with my shortcomings, and Cornelia Hamilton for discussions on the challenges of knitting and for her feedback on linguistic issues.

My warmest thanks to our models: Artíga, Birk, Niclas, Sofie, Susanne & Ayla the dog, Victoria and Viktor, lovely people from all walks of life, who have helped bring the garments to life.

The world is full of wonderful people who enter and exit my life; people who have visited the opening of the *Knitting Along the Viking Trail* exhibition, people attending workshops and lectures, colleagues from all over and people I've just bumped into, and who have generously shared tips about where to find patterns of the Viking cable type. Thank you for your thoughts, ideas, photos, links. Often I have received gifts in situations where I have been too stressed to ask for your names, so thank you all—I hope you know who you are; your help has been highly valued.

I owe a debt of gratitude to a number of friends who spent time and effort, and even involved their friends and colleagues, in order to help me gain some understanding of texts in German, Hungarian, Italian, Polish and Russian.

My sincere regard for all the fantastic people and institutions who post information on the Internet, making it possible to find knowledge that wasn't available just five years ago; collections made available online by museums and art collectors, old manuscripts published in facsimile in virtual libraries, new archeological finds described on the websites of institutions, doctoral theses from universities in other countries (the 657th search engine link led to a doctoral dissertation on shell gorgets), societies documenting their fields of interest, photographers posting their work on photosharing sites and so on and so on. Keep up the good work   you make life richer and more fun!

Last but not least, love and gratitude for my husband Anders, my playmate and collaborator, the love of my life. Your photography brings my design to life, your writing hones my thoughts with a humor and elegance I can only aspire to, and your lay-out skills combine them into a beautiful whole. Thank you for your strength when I am weak and your indulgence when I'm impossible. Your love gives life a deeper meaning.

Elsebeth Lavold